NEW BAMBOO
ARCHITECTURE AND DESIGN

MARCELO VILLEGAS

NEW BAMBOO
ARCHITECTURE AND DESIGN

Direction and edition
BENJAMÍN VILLEGAS

Coordination
LILIANA VILLEGAS

Texts
XIMENA LONDOÑO
MARCELO VILLEGAS
SIMÓN VÉLEZ
JESÚS VÉLEZ
GABRIEL GERMÁN LONDOÑO
GÖTZ SCHMITT

Villegas
editores

Book created, developed and edited
in Colombia by VILLEGAS ASOCIADOS S. A.
Avenida 82 No. 11-50, Interior 3
Bogotá, D. C., Colombia.
Telephone (57-1) 6161788
Fax (57-1) 6160020
e-mail: informacion@VillegasEditores.com

Design
BENJAMÍN VILLEGAS
LILIANA VILLEGAS

Art Department
HAIDY GARCÍA

English Translation
JIMMY WEISKOPF

Computer drawings
JAIME FRANCO
JORGE EDUARDO ARANGO
ALEJANDRO CARVAJAL

Mock-ups
RAFAEL MEJÍA

Photography
SIMÓN VÉLEZ
ANTONIO CASTAÑEDA
JORGE EDUARDO ARANGO
CRISTÓBAL VON ROTHKIRCH
MARCELO VILLEGAS
JESÚS VÉLEZ
OLGA LUCÍA NOVOA
JULIÁN VELÁSQUEZ
CARLOS B. ZETINA
LUIS GUILLERMO CAMARGO
ALEJANDRO CABO
BONNY FORERO
GLORIA P. CAMAYO
JOSÉ FERNANDO MACHADO
MAURICIO GUZMÁN
CIRECA
LILIANA VILLEGAS
ANGELINA FARIAS
RUDOLF
GERARDO REICHEL-DOLMATOFF
CLAUDIA URIBE TOURI
IRENE BOTERO
HUMBERTO CASTAÑO

First Edition, July 2003

ISBN 958-8156-06-8

VillegasEditores.com

Front Jacket
"Paloca"
Zicaru Huatulco Oaxaca, Mexico
Designed by Carlos Herrera, Jorge Herrera
and Simón Vélez

Back Jacket
Detail of furniture in guadua.
Designed by Marcelo Villegas

Page 1
The Guadua Pavilion, Manizales,
Caldas, Colombia
Designed by Simón Vélez

Page 2
Workshop of Marcelo Villegas
Manizales, Caldas, Colombia.

Pages 4/5
Guadua root.
Manizales, Caldas, Colombia.

Page 7
Microscopic view of vascular fiber sheath,
peripheral area and transitional zone of the
culm wall of *Guadua*.

Page 8
Alternative cathedral in guadua.
Pereira, Risaralda, Colombia.

The publisher wishes to express
special thanks to

CORPORACIÓN AUTÓNOMA
REGIONAL DEL VALLE DEL CAUCA

for the institutional sponsorship the
first edition of this book.

Contents

Foreword

BENJAMÍN VILLEGAS

In 1989 Villegas Editores published *Bambusa Guadua.* That book, which was a landmark, became an indispensable starting point for the subject, and not only in Colombia: it was the first large-scale book devoted to the characteristics of and possibilities for bamboo in the Western world. And as such it fulfilled its aim: it showed the world the best of native uses of this material, while also exploring new and unsuspected prospects for it.

Now, thirteen years later, this new book, *New Bamboo: Architecture and Design,* harvests the fruits of what was sown with the first one. Once again, it is a landmark, displaying the further evolution of the utilization of this plant and the findings of recent scientific and technical research. The architectural, industrial and design advances achieved with guadua have been prodigious.

Such feats owe much to Colombian specialists, like the architect Simón Vélez, the designer Marcelo Villegas and the scientist Ximena Londoño. Their persistence and achievements have enabled guadua to attain a leading role in the fight against poverty and underdevelopment.

Their work – which, we should point out, applies the results of their own original studies – has been made use of in more than eight countries, aside from Colombia.

When Expo-Hannover 2000, the great world's fair with which Germany inaugurated the new millennium, invited the international community to submit innovative proposals for guaranteeing a sustainable future for humanity, guadua was there. Its environmental friendliness, versatility of use, capacity to enrich the soil where it grows and potential as a sustainable resource had opened the doors.

Built entirely of guadua by Colombian workers in the middle of the harsh German winter, the Guadua Pavilion showed the world the visionary uses that are being made of this natural resource in our hemisphere. There in Hannover, people from every part of the planet saw the results of the stress and load tests to which the Pavilion had been subjected by German scientists. They were able to appreciate its capacity to span great spaces, the beauty it gives to architectural design, its virtues as a low-cost, easy to handle construction material – all of which have led it to be deservedly called the "vegetal steel". This, without mentioning its artistic and crafts possibilities and its great capacity to convert CO_2 into oxygen, which, under the carbon emissions swaps mechanisms of the Kyoto Protocol, may lead it to bring major earnings to the countries of Latin America.

For all of these reasons, we have no doubt in predicting that this book will be the first step towards a big contemporary boom in guadua. This material, traditional to the peasant-farmer culture of many Latin American countries, deserves to be restored to its rightful place, in the light of the new dimensions it has acquired through these recent breakthroughs. It will efficiently help to create employment, revitalize local economies and promote exports, needs that are shared by the developing world.

Detail of the structure of the main building. Puerto Peñalisa Girardot, Cundinamarca, Colombia. Designed by Simón Vélez.

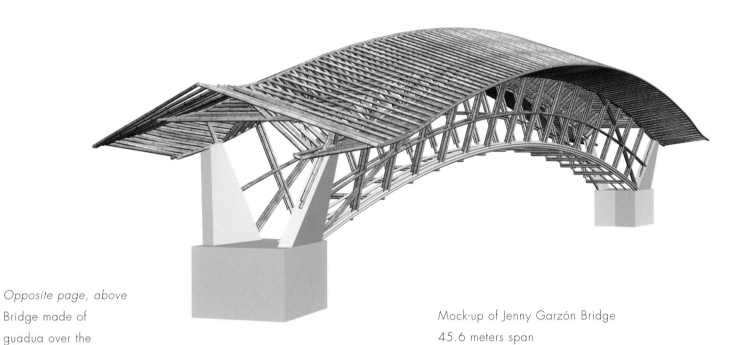

Opposite page, above
Bridge made of
guadua over the
Ingará river, 1853
Watercolor,
16.6 x 22.1 cm
Colombia

Mock-up of Jenny Garzón Bridge
45.6 meters span
Joint project: Bogotá Institute of Urban
Development, Sena (National Apprenticeship
Service) and Bambú de Colombia
Designed by Simón Vélez.

Opposite page, below
Bridge made of
guadua over the river
La Plata, 1857
Manuel M. Paz
Watercolor,
19.3 x 25.6 cm
Colombia

The watercolors on the
previous page
exemplify the principle
of "returning to the
future", that is,
combining a
traditional material
with contemporary
technology.

Right
Suspension bridge,
in which the guadua
is subjected to traction
stresses.
Tierradentro, Cauca,
Colombia.

Introduction

MARCELO VILLEGAS

The coffee zone of Colombia owed its development to guadua. Its houses, bridges, fences, aqueducts and coffee processing mills were built of guadua, part of an endless list of what guadua meant for the progress of this region.

When the first colonizers reached what is now the coffee zone of viejo Caldas, Valle del Risaralda and the outskirts of Pereira and Cartago in the Valle del Cauca, guadua was the predominant species.

Guadua was later displaced from the terrain by coffee plantations and pastures but in the past few years we have begun to see the zone reforested with guadua again.

This book seeks to show the new applications given to guadua.

One of its strongest possibilities – one that was unimaginable before the current world environmental crisis – is that guadua may bring economic benefits within a few years under the carbon emission trading mechanisms of the Kyoto Protocol, due to its capacity to capture CO_2 and convert it into oxygen, one of the planet's greatest needs and indispensable for our subsistence.

The guadua is of rapid growth and does not need a great deal of care.

The guadua has an optimum capacity to protect and improve the soil, since its extensive root system binds the soil together, which makes it irreplaceable for the protection of lands from erosion.

Guadua is a material that stands out by virtue of its structural properties. It is ideal for building, being light, highly resistant and easy to cut and transport.

Nowadays it is difficult to find an aqueduct made of guadua, but new and ingenious structures are being made with it. People are beginning to understand that guadua could be a viable economic alternative to coffee, which is currently in crisis in Colombia.

Wherever coffee haciendas are found, guadua has always been present in a wild form.

Desana fish trap, built in guadua by the Tukano Indians. Mandí region, river Vaupés, Colombia.

A sustainable timber resource of incalculable value

XIMENA LONDOÑO

The guadua, that gigantic and marvelous bamboo of America, is an extraordinary plant, thanks to its rapid growth, endurance, great versatility, lightness, resistance, flexibility, hollowness, easy handling and visual warmth. These qualities have given this *Gramineae* a leading role in the evolution of Latin American culture, specifically in countries like Colombia, Ecuador and Venezuela, where it has helped colonists to establish their towns and farmers to construct the infrastructure of their farms. It has also been used for traditional musical instruments and entered into the rural legends and myths of these countries.

The bamboo

The bamboos are the only group of *Gramineae* completely adapted to forests. Nevertheless it is not known if the bamboos and their immediate predecessors have always lived in forests or if they adapted to the forest habitat in a secondary way during the rapid diversification of the *Gramineae* that took place in the Oligocene-Miocene periods of the Tertiary era.

Due to their great adaptability, bamboos have a wide geographical range, which covers three large and well-defined regions. The first is the region of the Asian Pacific —the most extensive in area and the most advanced in the different aspects of the use and industrialization of bamboo. Then there is Africa and America.

The bamboos grow naturally in all continents, with the exception of Europe, from 51° North to 47° South, in latitudinal terms, and from sea level to 4,300 meters above sea level. Their maximum known altitude is found in the paramo or high moorlands of the equatorial Andes. Most bamboos prefer the humid habitats of the cloud forests and lowland tropical jungles, although some grow in dry but never desert habitats.

In all, 90 genera and 1100 species exist in the world, of which roughly half pertain to America — 41 genera and 451 species. They spread, in latitudinal terms, from the southeastern United States to southern Chile. The area with the highest degree of endemism and diversity in the region is Bahía, Brazil, followed by the cordillera of the Andes and the southern part of Central America.

In taxonomic terms, the bamboos belong to the *Poaceae* (or *Gramineae*) family and to the *Bambusoideae* subfamily. They are divided into two large groups: 1) the herbaceous bamboos or Olyreae, and 2) the woody bamboos or Bambuseae.

The herbaceous bamboos are joined in a single tribe, Olyreae, and their 100 species are grouped into 21 genera, 20 of them endemic to America: *Agnesia, Arberella, Cryptochloa, Diandrolyra, Ekmanochloa, Eremitis, Froesiochloa, Lithachne, Maclurolyra, Mniochloa, Olyra,*

Pariana, Piresia, Piresiella, Raddia, Raddiella, Rehia, Reitzia and *Sucrea*, and one from the Old World, *Buergersiochloa*.

These bamboos have rhizomes that are little-developed and culms (canes or stems) that are herbaceous or slightly lignified; are of short stature; show simple systems of ramification and a lack of cauline leaves; and have frequent but non-cyclical flowerings. Their preferred habitat is the herbaceous stratum of the tropical jungle and they are pollinated by insects. The range of herbaceous bamboos is from 29° latitude North to 34° latitude South, their greatest endemism and diversity being found between 10°-15° latitude North and South. They grow from sea level up to 1000 meters above sea level.

The woody bamboos tribe is divided into 9 sub-tribes, 3 of them endemic to America (Arthrostylidiinae, Chusqueinae and Guaduinae) and 5 to the Old World (Bambusinae, Nastinae, Melocanninae, Racemobambosinae and Shibataeinae); one, Arundariinae, is common to both.

They are characterized by having strong and well-developed rhizomes; lignified culms; new shoots protected by cauline leaves; complex systems of ramification; a lamina of deciduous foliage; cyclical and monocarpic flowerings; multi-flower spikelets; bisexual flowers arranged in spikelets or pseudo-spikelets; and a high range in the chromosomal number, with a basic value of $x = 12$. Their distribution, in terms of latitude and altitude, is the same as that of the sub-family. They grow in open habitats in which they are wind-pollinated and their diversity is associated with the radiation which reaches the different valleys and steep hillsides of cordilleras, mountains and ranges.

Of the American countries, Brazil shows the highest diversity, with a total of 141 species of woody bamboos. It is followed by Colombia, with 72 woody species; Venezuela, with 60; Ecuador, with 44; Costa Rica, with 39; and Mexico, with 37.

Due to the low economic value given to the resource of bamboo, there is no estimate of the areas covered by bamboo nor of its production in most Latin American countries. Nevertheless, there have been some attempts to make an inventory of them in countries like Colombia, Ecuador, Nicaragua and Venezuela. However, from satellite photos it has been calculated that in the southwestern part of the Amazon region, that is, in the frontier between the state of Acre in Brazil, Madre de Dios in Peru and Pando in Bolivia, the area covered by bamboos may be approximately 180,000 square kilometers. But, if we take into account that approximately 11% of each square kilometer of Andean forests is covered by bamboos, a possible estimate is that, at a minimum, 11 million hectares in Latin America are covered by bamboo.

Despite the fact that bamboo is an excellent renewable natural resource that could help to bring many economic, social and environmental benefits to the rural economies of Latin America, its use is limited to crafts work which is carried out by rural communities which exploit bamboo

forests that grow near their villages or farms. Only in countries like Colombia, Ecuador, Brazil and Costa Rica has bamboo had some degree of industrial development, above all in the field of construction and the manufacture of furniture and paper. It plays a conspicuous role in the local economies of, for example, the coffee zone of Colombia and the Pacific coast of Ecuador.

Guadua

In taxonomic terms, the guadua belongs to the family Poaceae, the sub-family Bambusoideae, the tribe Bambuseae, the sub-tribe Guaduinae and the genus *Guadua*.

The genus *Guadua* includes 30 species, which are spread from San Luis de Potosí in Mexico to Uruguay and northern Argentina, but are not found in Chile and the Caribbean islands.

45% of the species of the genus are of Amazonian origin. *Guadua weberbaueri* Pilger and *Guadua Sarcocarpa* Londoño & Peterson are the most frequent and abundant in the basin of this river. *Guadua paniculata* Munro shows the widest latitudinal range, which runs from Mexico to Brazil, and *Guadua Angustifolia* Kunth the widest spread of altitude, from sea level up to 2,600 meters above sea level.

The species of this genus may be distinguished from other bamboos mainly because of their long, thick and thorny culms; white bands of hairs in the region of the node and triangular-shaped cauline leaves. Nevertheless their most notable characteristics are the presence of winged keels in the palea of the floscule (floret) of the spikelet, the presence of three feathery stigmas at the end of the style, 6 stamens, stomata on both surfaces of the lamina of foliage and a chromosomal number of $2n = 46$.

Most species of the genus show an erect habit. However, species like *Guadua glomerata* Munro, *Guadua Macrospiculata* Londoño & Clark, *G. unicinata* Londoño & Clark, and *G. ciliata* Londoño & Davidse have a scandent or climbing habit. The culms of most species are hollow; however, *Guadua amplexifolia* Presl, *Guadua macrospiculata* Londoño & Clark, and *Guadua glomerata* have solid culms, a characteristic which gives them a good potential for use in the furniture or paper industry.

The potential uses of the different species of *Guadua* are infinite. In addition to the uses mentioned above, we may mention its role in the charcoal, crafts and pharmaceutical industries, among others.

The industrialization of guadua is a challenge that should be taken up in the twenty-first century, so that it may become a real source of economic, social and environmental benefits in Latin America.

Dense grove of guadua, with more than eight thousand stems per hectare. Quindío, Colombia

Guadua angustifolia

Of all the American bamboos the species *Guadua angustifolia* stands out. It is considered to be among the 20 best in the world by virtue of its physical-mechanical properties, great size and proven usefulness in the construction industry.

Guadua was described by the German botanist Kunth in 1822 as a genus segregated from the Asian one, *Bambusa*. Kunth used the indigenous word "guadua", which was the name given to this bamboo among the native communities of Colombia and Ecuador. He designated *Guadua angustifolia* as the species type, the specific epithet meaning "narrow leaf". Later, in 1868, Munro pointed out a series of its morphological characteristics and highlighted the very different

geographical distribution of these two taxa. In 1973, McClure decided that *Guadua* was a subgenus of *Bambusa*. However, after morphological, anatomical and molecular studies done by Soderstrom & Londoño (1987), Soderstrom & Ellis (1987) and Clark et. al. (1995), *Guadua* was clearly established as an endemic American genus.

Guadua angustifolia grows in its natural state in Colombia, Ecuador and Venezuela, where it forms dominant colonies known as "guaduales", mainly concentrated in the Andean region, between 0 and 2,000 meters above sea level. It is mostly seen on the banks of rivers and streams in the foothills of the cordillera, the middle and lower montane forests and inter-Andean valleys. *Guadua angustifolia* has been introduced to several Central American and Caribbean countries and even to Asia, North America and Europe.

Guadua angustifolia, bicolor variety with a great potential as an ornamental plant and good physical-mechanical properties. Quindío, Colombia.

In Colombia the "guaduales" or guadua groves reach their optimum development in the central region of the Andes, between 500 and 1,500 meters above sea level, at temperatures between 17 and 26° Centigrade, rainfalls of 1,200 – 2,500 mm/year, a relative humidity of 80 – 90% and on alluvial soils that are rich in volcanic ash with a moderate fertility and good drainage.

Up to now two varieties of the species have been reported for Colombia: *Guadua angustifolia* var. *bicolor* Londoño and *Guadua angustifolia* var. *nigra* Londoño. The guaduas known as "cebolla", "macana", "cotuda" and "castilla" seem to be ecotypes or forms that have to do with specific climatic and soil conditions. So far, molecular studies have indicated that the genetic diversity within this species is not significant and that the variations seem to be influenced by the eco-habitat. However, a high molecular diversity within the genus was shown.

In Colombia *Guadua angustifolia* has had a historical, cultural, economic and ecological tradition in the coffee zone, especially in the Departments (States) of Caldas, Quindío, Risaralda and Valle del Cauca. However, it is also found in the Departments of Antioquia, Boyacá, Cauca, Caquetá, Casanare, Cundinmarca, Chocó, Huila, Meta, Nariño, Norte de Santander, Putumayo, Santander and Tolima. It is estimated that at the present time it covers an area of 36,000 hectares in Colombia, of which 31,000 hectares are natural groves and 5,000 hectares cultivated ones. The coffee zone of Colombia, with 31,000 hectares of guadua groves, has the largest concentration.

Distribution of the species *Guadua Angustifolia* in South America, with the center in Colombian territory and extensions to Ecuador and Venezuela.

Because of its many virtues, this species enjoys a series of comparative advantages which make it more competitive than other resources in the implementation of sustainable productive systems.

Rhizome

In *G. angustifolia* the rhizome is of the pachymorphic kind with a pattern of sympodial ramification. The pachymorphic rhizomes usually have a short neck and their behavior is cespitose, as is the case with most of the Asian bamboos. However, *G. angustifolia* has rhizomes with necks that reach up to 1.5 meters in length, which reflects the spacing of the culms within the planta-

Opposite page
Guaduas in different stages of maturity: shoots and young, mature and dry specimens. Quindío, Colombia.

tion. This morphological characteristic facilitates its handling, especially in such aspects as the selection and cutting of the material.

In America the species *Guadua weberbaueri* shows the rhizome with the longest neck, 8 meters in length, a characteristic which makes it one of the species which most colonizes clearings in the jungle in the Amazon region.

Rapid growth

The bamboos in general, and *Guadua angustifolia* in particular, have a rapid growth and a higher productivity, when compared with trees. Generally, the guadua is ready to be utilized after 5 to 6 years of growth and if it is handled properly, it may have an unlimited production once it has been established. Usually, the growth cycle of a bamboo is a third of that of a tree of rapid growth and its productivity per hectare is twice that of a tree. In addition, bamboos emerge from the soil with a fixed diameter, without showing increases of diameter over time, as happens with trees. The maximum diameter reported for *Guadua angustifolia* is 25 cm and the average is between 9 and 13 centimeters.

In the case of *Guadua angustifolia*, a 21 cm daily growth in height has been observed, so that it reaches its maximum height (15 – 30 meters) in the first six months of growth and its maturity at 5 to 6 years. This growth is rarely surpassed by the native timber species of the region. The ideal composition of culms in a guadua grove is estimated to be 10% shoots, 30% young ones, 60% mature and over-mature ones and 0% dry ones, with a density of 3000 to 8000 culms per hectare, there being an inverse relation between density and average diameter. The per hectare productivity of this species is 1,200 – 1,350 culms per hectare per year.

Guadua angustifolia is an effective alternative to wood and like other bamboos may industrially yield every kind of laminated and agglomerate wood (columns, beams, girders, planks, panels, etc.).

It is only through reforestation programs sponsored by state institutions and the establishment of its credibility among farmers that this bamboo will become a viable economic alternative.

Below
Inflorescence of
Guadua angustifolia.
Quindío, Colombia.

Opposite page
Guadua grove where
you see the plant in a
mature state.
Valle del Cauca,
Colombia.

Flowering

The phenomenon of flowering in bamboos has captivated the imagination of all those who are interested in this plant and in the evolutionary ecology of plant populations.

The precise functioning of the factor of time and the mechanism that works on a molecular level to control the flowering of bamboos is still unknown. Florescence in bamboos may be gregarious, sporadic or continual. Gregarious flowerings are those which occur at regular intervals and generally only once in the lifetime of the plant. This type of florescence is usually followed by the mass death of the individuals, populations or species and shows cycles of flowering that may vary, from species to species, between 2 and 100 years. The large majority of woody bamboos that show this type of florescence die after flowering.

Sporadic flowerings are those which occur at irregular intervals, with or without the death of the plant. *Guadua angustifolia* has this type of florescence, with the peculiarity that it does not die after flowering and flourishes annually, which is generally associated with hot summers. In plantations with gregarious flowering one has to renew the cultivation after every florescence, while in plantations of *Guadua angustifolia* sustainability over time is perennial.

Environmental advantages

The guadua provides countless environmental services. It conserves the soil, controls erosion, regulates the flow of rivers and streams, supplies organic material, and contributes to biodiversity by offering a habitat to diverse flora and fauna. It also acts as CO_2 sink and embellishes the landscape, thus serving to encourage eco-tourism.

Its rapid growth, both aerial and sub-surface, the network of rhizomes that grow in the superficial layer of the soil (20 – 50 centimeters) and its willingness to occupy disturbed areas make guadua an ideal resource for the conservation of unstable soils. By providing shade and a covering of dry leaves, guadua has been used to protect the surface of the soil from solar action and recuperate lands that have been degraded through deforestation and inefficient agricultural practices

Guadua groves are ecosystems which harbor diverse flora, micro-flora, entomo-fauna, mammals, birds, reptiles and amphibians. More than 120 plant species, 48 bird species, 20 mammal species and 7 reptile species associated with guadua groves have been recorded.

The mere fact that guadua culms may be exploited by their transformation into material for housing, furniture, crafts, etc., makes this bamboo a plant that fixates CO_2 .

By virtue of being, for the most part, developing ones, the countries of Latin America are not bound by commitments to reduce greenhouse-effect gases and they may thus benefit from international carbon emission swaps through the mechanisms for clean development laid down in the Kyoto Protocol.

Recent studies indicate that the potential for atmospheric carbon dioxide fixation in the first six years of *G. Angustifolia*'s growth from new sowings is 54 metric tons per hectare – a fundamental discovery that facilitates participation in the international system of trading emission rights and will bring additional benefits to the investors and farmers who plant and cultivate guadua.

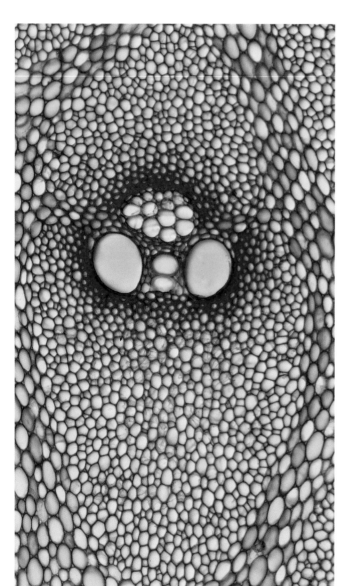

Quality of fiber

The very strong natural fibers of the *Guadua angustifolia* make it among the 20 best species of bamboo in the world. It has been demonstrated that with this fiber one may develop industrialized products such as panels (plywood, laminates, floors), houses and handicrafts.

It is important to point out that using guadua in these industrial processes would significantly reduce negative environmental impacts on native forests, since guadua becomes a substitute for timber, thus reducing the pressure on the tropical jungle. In addition, it would generate a demand for manpower in rural zones where there is a lot of unemployment.

Bamboo panels, especially floors, are more and more in demand all over the world, because they have the tex-

Microscopic view of the vascular sheath of *Guadua angustifolia* (100x). Laboratory of Cenicafé (National Coffee Research Center) Chinchiná, Caldas, Colombia.

ture of marble and the elegance of wood; in addition, they are strong, durable, smooth, clean, non-sliding and resistant to humidity.

The properties of bamboo culms are determined by their anatomical structure and these anatomical characteristics of the culm are reflected in the final use of the material. The composition of the tissues in a culm of *G. Angustifolia* is 40% fiber, 51% parenchyma and 9% conductive tissue.

The fiber content is higher in the apical segment (56%) than in the middle (26%) and base (29%) segments.In comparison with other tropical and subtropical bamboos,this species shows a relatively high percentage of fiber and a higher content of silica in the epidermis, which explains its astonishing strength and flexibility.

Anatomy

In anatomical terms, a bamboo is composed of a cortex, parenchyma, fibers and vascular bundles. The shape, size, number and concentration of vascular bundles vary from the periphery to the internal part.

In *Guadua angustifolia* a cross-section of the culm wall shows four zones: a) the peripheral zone, which is between 0.67-0.77 mm long and is composed of vascular bundles immediately adjacent to the cortex or outer skin; these bundles are small, circular and numerous, with little conductive tissue and few parenchymatous cells. b) the transitional zone, which is between 1.23-2.55 mm long and accounts for 10% of the thickness of the culm wall. c) the central or middle zone, which is between 4.95-16.34 mm long and accounts for 56% of the thickness of the culm wall. And, d) the inner zone, which is between 1.3-2 mm long and accounts for 12% of the thickness of the culm wall.

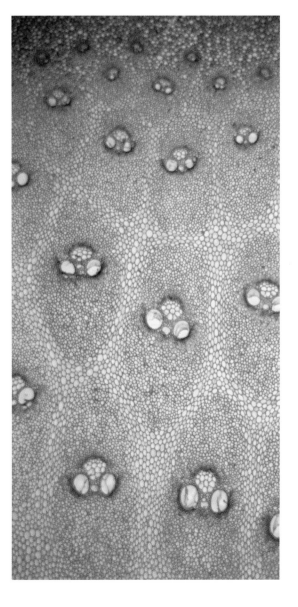

Microscopic view of cross section of culm of *Guadua angustifolia* (40x). Laboratory of Cenicafé (National Coffee Research Center) Chinchiná, Caldas, Colombia.

Building material

The species *Guadua angustifolia* stands out within the genus by virtue of its structural properties, such as its strength/weight ratio, which surpasses that of most woods and may even be compared to steel and some high-tech fibers. Its capacity to absorb energy and allow for higher bending strength makes this bamboo an ideal material for seismic-resistant constructions

You can erect monumental building with guadua, like the Guadua Pavilion designed and constructed by the Colombian architect Simón Vélez in the Expo Hannover Fair in Germany in 2000, where visitors from all over the world saw the potential of this wonderful material. But, above all, guadua offers the possibility of building low-cost housing, which is the reason why it is known as the "poor man's wood". The new construction technologies with this material, which have been achieved thanks to the efforts of Colombian and Ecuadorian architects and engineers, have made it possible for houses built of guadua to meet the requirements of low cost, an aesthetic appearance and a safe and rapid construction. After the earthquake which struck Colombia's coffee zone in 1999 several plans were developed in Colombia for housing the victims of the quake in buildings made of guadua. In Ecuador, after the damage caused by el Niño phenomenon of 1998, up to 80 prefabricated houses made of guadua were constructed daily, to make up for the shortage of housing caused by that natural disaster.

The cost of building with guadua is much lower than that of using conventional materials: it is up to 45% cheaper. For that reason this resource has become a real alternative for helping to solve, in an economic way, the serious problems caused by the shortage of housing in most Latin American countries.

It is necessary to continue developing construction technologies that simplify and universalize the use of this material as an element in building. In addition to being a renewable natural resource of quick growth and easy handling, guadua is suitable for multiple architectural uses.

House.
Riosucio, Caldas,
Colombia.

Multiple uses

Guadua has countless applications in the daily life of rural inhabitants: they include musical instruments, domestic utensils, handicrafts, furniture, tools and even farm infrastructure.

Nowadays crafts and furniture made of guadua have modern and innovative designs. These crafts products are attractive to tourists and are daily turning into export goods that are in great demand. It is indispensable to dry and immunize the guadua used in such products so that they can meet international phyto-sanitary and environmental requirements.

The commercial activity resulting from the exploitation of guadua in the regions where it grows has created direct and indirect benefits for guadua cultivators, the transport industry, farmers, craftsmen, builders, industrialists and estate-owners, among others, which has led to a growing demand for guadua in the Colombian market and prospects for sales to overseas markets.

In the light of all these advantages, it is necessary to involve guadua in systems of sustainable agricultural production, continue research into its uses, advance its industrialization and convert it into a viable economic alternative that will principally benefit rural communities

Guadua is a natural material with an incalculable potential which may, at the same time, bring economic, social and environmental benefits that are key to the integral development of the countries of Latin America.

"Chicken foot" structure for a brick works.
Caicedonia, Valle, Colombia.

Marginal
neighborhood, built
of guadua in less
than a month.
Manizales, Caldas,
Colombia.

Coffee drying shed, built at the end of the 19th century. This building is one of the few surviving examples of a typical feature of coffee haciendas until the arrival of new drying techniques. The whole four-storey structure is built in guadua. The absence of walls allows air to circulate through the structure. It has a four-slope roof, wooden floors and railings of *macana*-wood.
Hacienda Cascarero, on the banks of the river Guacaica. Lisboa, Caldas, Colombia.

Hacienda Nápoles
Pereira, Risaralda,
Colombia.

The fauna of the guadua grove

JESÚS VÉLEZ

Guadua groves occupy areas where the tropics overflow with life, for which reason they constitute excellent refuges for wild life. Their enormous size and perennial vegetation provide optimum conditions for the development of a great number of animals, since differences in light and humidity favor associations with other plant communities.

Unfortunately there are very few studies of the fauna associated with guadua groves. Many studies are limited to the taxonomic inventories realized by different specialists, but if we pause to observe the groves, as an ordinary spectator, we may discover a great number of living beings, both vertebrates and invertebrates.

Among the former, the easiest to spot are the birds, which on occasions form veritable colonies in the groves. An example is the cattle egret, which carries out its whole life cycle in the guadua grove. Its presence is a bother for humans at times, due to the odor produced by its guano or some dead chick that decomposes on the ground, but these colonies attract a number of predators like serpents, *babillas* (caimans), lizards, etc. We also see colonies of *arrendajos* or caciques (*cacicus sp.*), which weave their nests in the form of a pouch, one next to another, and are associated with nests of wasps (Hymenoptera), which protect them from predators. Another group of birds that are highly visible because of the uproar they make are the parrots (Psittacidae), who not only use the guaduas as dormitories but also as nests, taking advantage of the hollows in the internodes of old canes.

Above
Catharus ustulatus
Swainson's Thrush.

Below
Atlapetes schistaceus.

When there are growths of grasses or other plants that serve as forage around the guaduas, we will see several species of turtledoves (Columbidae) feeding and even nesting in the foliage, which attracts a number of predators, like hawks and falcons, whose large nests made of twigs may be seen in the bigger guaduas.

In the interior of the grove we may observe a few tinamous and pheasants forming family groups. You also hear the resonant vocalizations of *guacharacas* (or chachalacas) and wild turkeys. Cuckoos and tick-hunters are frequently seen and even nest here, since they find many of the insects that make up their diet. It is easy to spot hummingbirds (*Amazilia, Anthracothorax*) and various *Phaethornis* or hermit hummingbirds inside the groves.

Barranquillos (*Momotus*) and toucans (Ramphastidae) also visit the groves, as well as a large number of birds and insectivores, among which false woodpeckers, wrens and antbirds stand out, since it is a strategic feeding site by virtue of the great number of insects that are found there.

These are some of the bird species that we observe in the guadua grove. Their numbers increase when the grove is joined to native forests, a situation where, on occasions, mixed groups of birds numbering up to 15 species use it as a bridge in their search for food

For the most part, mammals are hard to see, by virtue of their solitary or nocturnal habits. The groves attract many animals which have sharply marked territories, from the ground to the upper foliage. In the lower part, we find a number of rodents, like the *guatines*, who frequently appear along the tracks. The *guaguas* (or agoutis), the world's second biggest rodent, occasionally make their nests and burrows by the side of streams. Unfortunately, along with the *guatines* they have been nearly exterminated from the guadua groves of the coffee belt, due to hunters who pursue them with dogs. Mice are rather difficult to classify and of the rodent group the most common species are squirrels. They are frequently caught in the traps set by researchers. This habitat attracts many bats, above all insectivorous ones, since a great number of moths and other bugs are found there. The armadillos are often hunted down, for their meat and also because of the false idea that their blood cures asthma. They are found in big burrows, on occasions near colonies of *arrieras*, or leaf-cutting ants.

Foxes prowl about these sites, in search of rodents, insects or chicks. Where they are not hunted down a lot, *chuchas* (opossums) find a safe refuge.

A number of primates may be seen in the guadua grove. The biggest of all is the howler monkey (*Allovata*), which forms numerous clans: their loud cries give them away. The tiny

Above
Cyclarhis nigrirostris,
Black-billed
Peppershrike.

Below, left
Mountain paca
Agouti taczanowskii.

Below, right
Dasypus novemcinctus.

monkeys known as *titíes* are frequently seen, along with a number which belong to threatened species of the Saguinus genus. Many of these seek out insects and resins in tree trunks.

A number of carnivores venture into the groves, looking for eggs, chicks or some mammal in the burrows. Among these are the felines known as the *tigrillo* and the *yaguarondí*.

In areas that are little disturbed we see the sloth (*Bradypus sp.*), a slow-moving animal that hangs from the branches and only descends from his tree in order to defecate. At times the porcupine (*Coendu sp.*) betrays his presence, an animal of nocturnal habits with a prehensile tail, which gives off a strong odor and feeds off tender leaves, flowers, fruits and seeds.

A very interesting inhabitant of the guadua grove is the *marteja* or night monkey (*Aotus sp*), the only nocturnal primate, which we may see sleeping in a big hole in family groups.

At times we only see the mammals associated with the foliage when they upset a wasps nest or beehive in their wandering, with unfortunate consequences in the way of stings, or betray their presence to some winged predator.

Reptiles like lizards, some large like the iguana and the basilisk, sun themselves on branches. Serpents, some of them climbing ones, are attracted by the opportunity to feed off chicks, baby mammals, rodents and bats. There are also several kinds of toads and tree frogs, which betray their presence by their mating songs.

Insects make up the group that is most abundant in species. They have adapted themselves to almost all ecosystems and their maximum representation is in the tropics.

Nevertheless, there are very few studies of the entomofauna of the guadua groves and we lack a complete register of the insects that may be found in this environment. But we do know that the principal orders are found there, like the Coleoptera (beetles), Lepodoptera (butterflies), Hymenoptera (wasps), Dipters (flies), Odonata (dragonflies) and Orthoptera (crickets): among these the lepidopters or butterflies stand out, since they are the best known and the most prominent order after the coleopters. Some carry out the whole of their metamorphosis in the guadua grove, as in the case of a number of Hesperids, since it is their host plant. Within the grove we may observe, as permanent inhabitants, a number of satyrids of the genus *Pierella Caerois* and a number of *Taygetis*.

A number of Morphus butterflies fly along the borders or in the depths of the groves, where they are frequently caught by jacamars (*Galbula sp*), which are a sort of big hummingbird.

Above
Tropical Screech Owl
Otus choliba

Below
Ocelot
Leopardus pardalis

Many of the ithodmids fly in the broken light and shadows of the grove, at time in large groups, forming a unique spectacle, since they are a butterfly species with crystalline wings, due to the absence of scales.

The Brassolinae known as "owl's eyes" because of the markings on the undersides of their wings, are protected in the depths of the grove. The Heliconiidae associated with Passiflora, like the passionfruits known as *curubos* and *granadillos*, flutter in and out of the grove, searching for a place to lay their eggs. Many nymphalids rest on the guadua stems, like the Prepona, Hamadryad, Memphis and Consul butterflies. These are some of the many butterflies which are associated with the guadua grove, attracted by its fresh, humid climate and seeking refuge there from the hours of hot sun. There are no specialized studies in this country about the lepidopters which take advantage of the benign environment that this magnificent plant provides.

The conservation of all of these species depends on the preservation not only of the guadua grove but also of the native forests that surround them, since the latter provide shelter and food for all these species. Their protection depends on further studies, which will show what measures must be taken to enable them to continue to be symbols of biodiversity.

Left
Green Violet-Ear
Hummingbird
Colibri thalassinus

Right, above
Butterfly
Pteronimia lisae.

Right, below
Butterfly
Pteronymia veia.

Guadua, the vegetal steel

SIMÓN VÉLEZ

The subject of this book is Guadua, the poor man's wood, the most common and ordinary of all of our construction materials and at the same time, the most extraordinary one. It defines our culture and the landscape of the region where I was born, Manizales.

A little under a hundred years ago, concrete appeared as a construction material. Cement is millenary and iron as well.

But the historically-recent combination of these two materials caused the biggest revolution ever known in the technology of construction. Before the appearance of concrete, architecture was worked within the limitations of known materials: adobe, brick, rammed earth, stone, mortar, wood, iron. These limitations forced people to construct within technical traditions that had been enshrined by the experience accumulated over many generations. These building techniques were as ancient as language and wound up becoming in themselves another language for every culture.

We can recognize a culture by its buildings: Greek, Egyptian, Japanese, Spanish, etc. Just as there are no ugly languages, neither were there ugly architectures. For the first time in history architecture has stopped being one of the fine arts and become the ugliest art of all. When I travel round the world, all of the buildings built before the appearance of concrete, whether they are elitist or popular, I find beautiful. The constructional possibilities of concrete are so unlimited that the human scale is abandoned at once. Without limitations you cannot speak nor listen to a language. It would be as though, in order to converse, we all used loudspeakers and spoke at the same time. Concrete bewildered architecture.

Twenty years ago, I got interested in making a small structure in guadua. My previous experience of working with wood did not help in the case of a material that is so different.

I wanted to build a cantilever roof that would stand the stress of traction but I could not find a way to make a joint for a hollow material like guadua. One day, it suddenly occurred to me that if I filled with cement the

Salt-lick shed. The first structure in guadua with a concrete joint for traction. Pereira, Risaralda, Colombia.

inter-node chamber where the joint was, which in turn would have iron bolts, it might work. And it did.

This was a technical discovery that radically changed my work as a designer and builder, just as concrete had in the history of construction. On the basis of this concrete joint in the inter nodes of guadua, mainly to deal with the stresses of traction but also with those of compression, guadua became a veritable vegetal steel for me.

Guadua is a high-technology material: Its weight/strength ratio surpasses that of steel. In environmental terms, there is no subject more charismatic than guadua.

Our experience with the Guadua Pavilion in Expo-Hannover 2000 has opened up many possibilities: an unrestricted construction license was obtained from the world's strictest authorities for a structural material and structural techniques that were unknown to the Germans.

Drawing on our enormous bio-ethnic diversity, Colombia, a country on the periphery of the tropical third world, is now able to create enriching proposals for construction without the slightest inferiority complex.

"Caballo Loco" Bar. One of the first arched structures made in guadua. Manizales, Caldas, Colombia.

Pages 46/47 Guadua grove that covers and protects the course of a stream. Obando, Valle del Cauca, Colombia.

Alternative cathedral in guadua. Built as a temporary replacement for the cathedral of Pereira, "Nuestra Señora de la Pobreza" (Our Lady of Poverty), which was being remodeled. Pereira, Risaralda, Colombia.

That raft, that river and that hope

GABRIEL GERMÁN LONDOÑO

It happened a short time after the playing of the Colombian national anthem and the raising of the Colombian flag in some plaza of Beijing announced to the world that we were recognized as a member country of the INBAR (International Network for Bamboo and Rattan, whose seat is in Beijing).

In another plaza, the Bolívar Plaza of Pereira, I negotiated, in the midst of chats with the Bishop of the Diocese, the number of full indulgences that the soul of Simón Vélez would need to reach heaven. That morning I had seen the first sketches for an Alternative Cathedral in guadua which the maestro Veléz had drawn on some breakfast napkins as he told me several times that, taking advantage of the curves which the guadua naturally forms in the groves, you could easily achieve the arches of Gothic cathedrals. Monsignor, I told him: indulgences or not, all of the consultants for this Cathedral will go to heaven without restrictions, because we have just discovered that God invented the guadua so that churches could be built to honor Him. And God invented it with such delight and for so many purposes and immortalized it and imbued it with so much love that He made it adorable.

Guadua has grown in this region of the coffee belt forever and for that reason has played a fortunate role in the lives of its inhabitants over the past millennia. It was only by taking advantage of the high temperature of guadua charcoal that the ancient Quimbaya Indians were able to perfect the fusion of gold that made their gold pieces unsurpassable. And of guadua were the cages that the ancient Calima Indians invented to guard the great amount of fish that they caught during the floodtides of the River Cauca. And their thatched huts – whether ceremonial long houses or simple homes – were built and rebuilt in guadua for endless centuries. It was in 1850 that the colonizers of Antioquia, fleeing from wars and seeking their fortunes, confronted the immense jungles of guadua and felled them to create the paradigms of wealth that still endure today: coffee, cattle, sugar cane, plantain, maize, cassava. Millions of hectares of wild guadua groves thus disappeared, excèpt for the few that were preserved, here and there, on farms, where the guadua became an indispensable building material. It provided posts for barbed-wire fences, fencing for animal enclosures and props for plantain trees. It was used to fix leaking roofs and burned as fuel in the kitchens. But, most important, sufficient groves survive to open the eyes and warm the hearts of many people today and also awaken the interest of the government, and we are beginning to rediscover, with gratitude, the immense virtues of this colossal resource. We are still fleeing from wars and we once more seek our fortunes in guadua. We have planted a guadua grove for industrial purposes whose area is so large that only the ancient Quimbayas knew its like. And we have accepted the invitation of the maestro Jorge Robledo, one of whose verses asks us "to build of bamboo rafts of fantasy to ascend a river of hope."

Dear reader. This book is that raft, that river and that hope.

The alternative
cathedral in guadua,
with an area of 700
square meters, was
constructed in five
weeks at a cost of
30,000 dollars. The
technique built on the
experience obtained
in the use of curved
guaduas in the
nurseries of
Santagueda, Caldas,
whose design had
been inspired by the
natural vaults formed
by the guadua groves
that border the streams
of the region.
Pereira, Risaralda,
Colombia.

Alternative cathedral
in guadua.
Pereira, Risaralda,
Colombia.

Only drawing used to
give instructions to the
workers and
solicit the construction
license for this
alternative cathedral.
The bureaucratic
tyranny that requires
an architect to present
hundreds of useless
drawings in order to
get his projects
approved is the
nightmare that has
forced Simón Vélez to
work, in many cases,
as a rural architect.

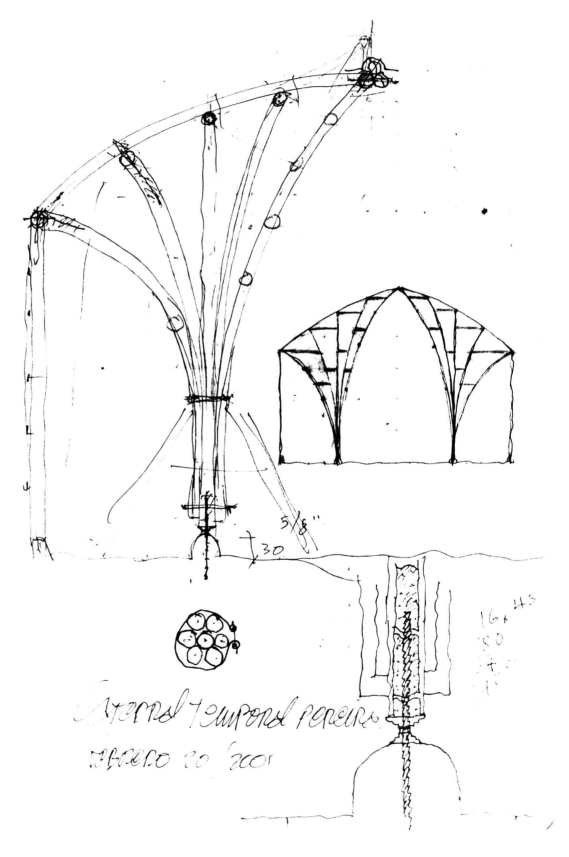

The Guadua Pavilion

MARCELO VILLEGAS

This pavilion, which has the geometrical shape of a ten-sided polygon, has a constructed area of 2000 square meters. Its roof is a guadua structure topped by a cement mortar that is waterproofed with a mantle upon which the ceramic roof tiles are placed.

This cantilever roof has a weight of 200 kg/ square meter, seventy percent of which is made up of overhangs that reach a 7.50 meters span on ground level. The pavilion has a mezzanine of 550 square meters, with a massive concrete slab, 10 cm thick, which rests on forty columns, each made up of bunches of six trunks of *aliso*-wood, tied together with iron clamps.

These columns rest on steel ball and socket joints, anchored to a concrete base that keeps the wood from touching the ground. Guadua roots are used to form arches which transfer the stresses to the *aliso*-wood columns, by means of joints with steels bolts that allow for the post-tensing of the forces that occur when the diameters of the columns shrink as they dry.

The main criterion in the design of this structure was to only use the different varieties of timber and bamboo that naturally grow in this region, whether they are fine or ordinary woods.

The columns of *aliso* bunches use a very low density wood that has never been employed in building for structural purposes. According to Simón Vélez, if the trunk of any plant that has the bearing of a tree has the strength to put up with the impact of wind and rain against its foliage, it necessarily serves as a structural wood for building, no matter whether it is considered to be a fine or ordinary wood. As Vélez declares, "not even in botany can you be a racist."

The Guadua Pavilion.
Manizales, Caldas,
Colombia.

Manizales, Colombia

54

Physical stress tests

MARCELO VILLEGAS

Before giving their authorization to build the structure of guadua for the Pavilion at the Expo 2000 World's Fair at Hannover, the German authorities required a pavilion exactly like the one that would be erected in Germany to be built in Colombia, so that it would serve as a model for the physical stress tests in the absence of previous studies to determine the mechanical and physical properties of guadua.

This gap was temporarily filled by using the degree thesis of Jenny Garzón, architect from the Universidad Nacional de Colombia (National University of Colombia), who investigated the resistance of the structural joints developed by Simón Vélez for his guadua buildings. All of her findings were later confirmed by the studies done in Germany.

Professor Klaus Steffens – director since 1980 of the Institute of Experimental Statics of the University of Bremen – has realized experimental evaluations of load bearing and safety for the reconstruction of the Reichstag building in Berlin, among others; he designed the following load bearing tests, in order to determine the bearing capacity of this pavilion.

1. Consisted of determining the load bearing capacity of the cantilevers (a 7.30 meters overhang). This was done by hanging a weight of more than 650 kilograms in the middle third of their spans. A deformation of 7 millimeters was observed, which the structure recovered when it was freed of the burden.

2. To test the capacity of the upper floor, this structure was loaded down with 55-gallon barrels, which were uniformly spread over the surface and filled with water until they reached a load of 400 kilograms per square meter. When the deformation of the upper floor under this burden was measured, it came to 5 millimeters, which were recovered when the weight was removed. It is important to note that the estimated

Load bearing test, with barrels full of water (400kg/square meter), on the second floor.

Professor Klaus
Steffens, Simón Vélez
and Marcelo Villegas
during the realization
of the load bearing
tests in the Guadua
Pavilion.
Manizales, Caldas,
Colombia.

deformation for this test was expected to reach 25 millimeters, which means that the result was a fifth of the estimate.

3. The third test involved a simulation of wind stresses and consisted of pulling the structure in a horizontal direction. This was done by placing one cable in the middle part and another in the upper part of each one of the pediments of the pavilion and then subjecting each cable to a horizontal load of five tons. The result obtained was a horizontal displacement of one centimeter.

After carrying out these tests in Manizales, Professor Steffens issued a technical assessment that helped to support the application for the construction permit that was granted for the pavilion in the Hannover Expo-2000 fair. This study was complemented by a structural calculation carried out by Professor Joseph Lindemann, an estimate that was based, in part, on the results of traction, compression and flexion tests done by him in Germany. Thus guadua passed all the tests and was officially authorized for architectural use in one of the countries with the strictest construction codes in the world.

Certification of the tests

KLAUS STEFFENS

Only a few days are left!
EXPO 2000 HANNOVER

The bamboo pavilion is nearly finished. Only one step is lacking for this bold and gigantic mushroom designed by the Colombian architect Simón Vélez to start functioning on June 1, 2000, but it is a definitive one: Testing its safety!

The normal method, which only employs static calculus, was not possible, because the materials, joining points and the quality of workmanship cannot be measured with sufficient reliability. In such cases, German construction norms offer a special solution, which applies to this particular case: an authorization to carry out load bearing tests on the original building.

Between May 9 and 12, 2000, The Bremen IInstitute of Experimental Statics (Hochschule Bremen Institut für Experimentelle Statik - IFES), under the supervision of the engineer Professor Klaus Steffens, will carry out load bearing tests on the most important parts of the pavilion's structure. With the use of hydraulic load instruments test loads of up to 25 tons will be applied in a vertical and horizontal direction, simulating stresses produced by use, snow and storms. A number of electric sensors and a very modern technique of computerized measurement will measure the reactions of the building and show them on the monitor.

If you are interested in this unusual event, please get in touch with the secretariat of the Institute of Experimental Statics to arrange an appointment (Mrs. Röwer, telephone: 0421-59052345)

Bremen, 05-03-2000

Engineer
J. Lindemann,
Lange Lambe 19, 30150
Hannover, Fax 0049 511 196 66

Dear Mr. Lindemann:

I enclose the original results of the tests done to the cantiliver roofs and the galleries. The deformations are surprisingly minimal and totally reversible without slow flow, even in the case of a continuous load.

In general, the building gives the impression of great solidity. There is no doubt that the pavilion will have no problems in Hannover, if it is done with the same quality. The execution of the manual work here is higher than the German standard. It seems to have the quality of fine carpentry!

Tomorrow we will do the horizontal test. Afterwards there will be a celebration! My presence here was necessary. There might not have been any progress this week without the general coordination of the tests that I carried out.

I am going to recommend, without hesitation, a rapid issuing of the partial construction permit, independently of Stuttgart, so that we are not vulnerable to setbacks through a lack of time.

Best wishes,

KLAUS STEFFENS

Manizales 11-04-1999

English translation of the original letter, written in German by the engineer Steffens, a facsimile of which appears on the opposite page.

Steffens, Manizales 04. 11. 1999

Herrn
Dipl.-Ing. J. Lindemann
Lange Laube 10, 30159 Hannover

Fax 0049 511 186 66

3 Anlagen

Sehr geehrter Herr Lindemann,
anbei die originalen Ergebnisse der Test an den Kragdächern und der Empore. Die Verformungen sind erstaunlich gering und voll reversibel ohne Kriechanteil auch bei Dauerlast.

Insgesamt macht die Konstruktion einen sehr soliden Eindruck. Ich habe keinen Zweifel, daß bei gleicher Ausführungsqualität des Pavillon in Hannover keinerlei Probleme bereitet. Die Ausführung der handwerklichen Arbeiten ist besser als deutscher Standard – eher Tischlerqualität!

Morgen werden wir noch den Horizontalversuch machen. Dann wird gefeiert!

Meine Anwesenheit hier war zwingend – ohne meine komplette Versuchsleitung wäre hier wohl in dieser Woche nichts gelaufen.
Insgesamt kann ich eine rasche Freigabe der Teilbaugenehmigung unabhängig von Stuttgart nur empfehlen, damit wir nicht an der Zeit scheitern! Grüße K. St.

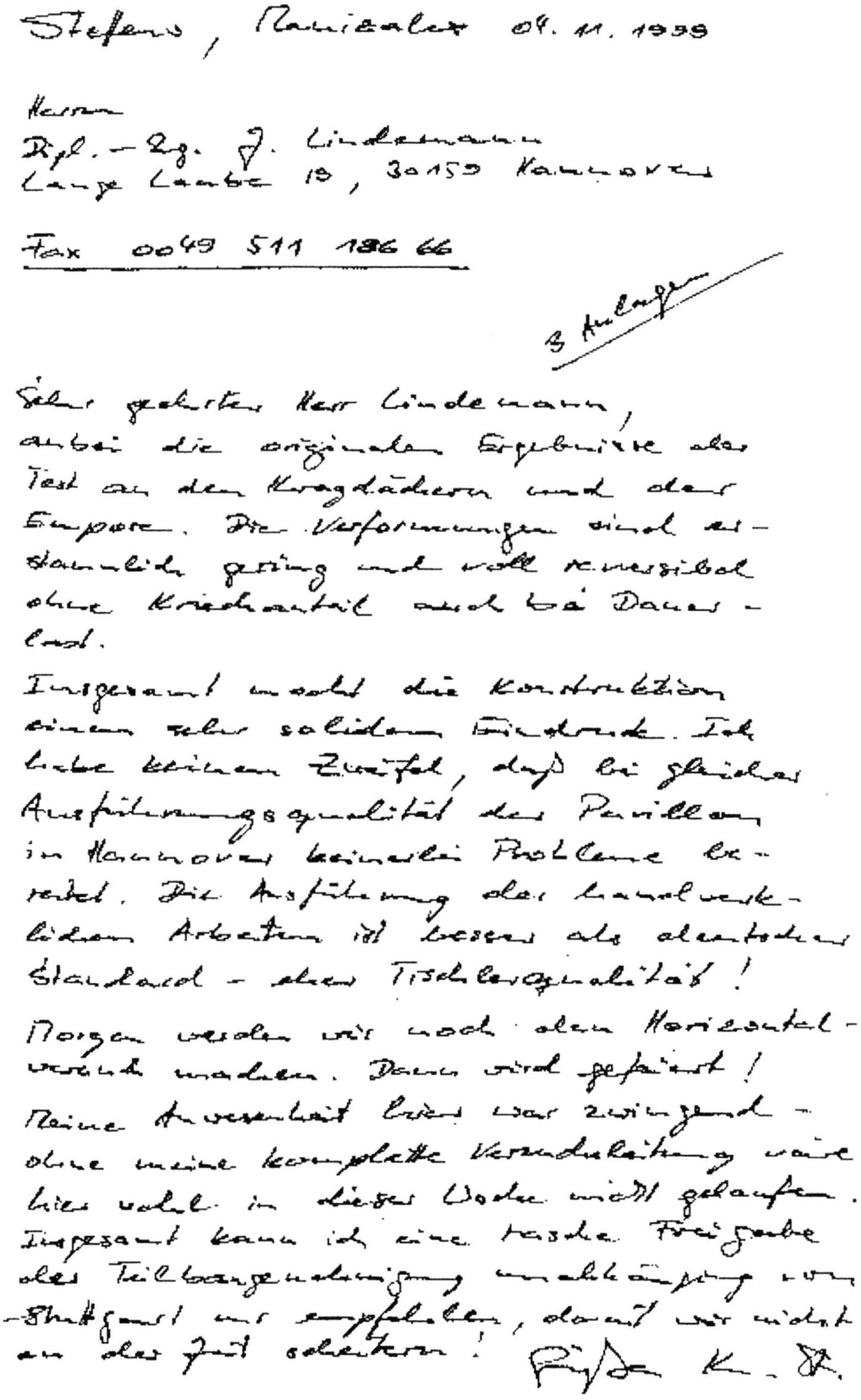

Facsimile of the manuscript of the letter sent to Germany by the engineer Klaus Steffens, in which he notes and comments on the results of the tests done to the guadua pavilion in Manizales.

Hannover, Germany

Above
Expo-Hannover 2000, in Germany, was the world´s fair that marked the beginning of the new millennium. It showed the world a new global vision of the future, offering practical examples for improving the life of the six billion people who co-inhabit the earth and models for restoring the equilibrium between man, nature and technology. Among the proposals for establishing a sustainable and lasting development, the Guadua Pavilion, designed by Simón Vélez, appears in the photo with the roof still unfinished. Another, seen beside it, was the Japanese Pavilion, designed by Shigeru Ban, with its great white plastic roof.

Below
Ceremony inaugurating the Guadua Pavilion at Expo-Hannover 2000.

Above

The construction, in mid winter, of the Guadua Pavilion required a tenacious effort on the part of the Colombian workers who traveled to Hannover for the job.

Below

In the background, behind the construction work on the Guadua Pavilion, we see the tubular structure made of recycled cardboard, reinforced with a framework of wood and steel, of the Japanese Pavilion.

Pages 64-65

Detail of the ridgepole of the Guadua Pavilion, where the structural trunks join.

Page 66

Detail of the structure of the Liquid Jungle Laboratory. Panama. Design: Marco Zanini

Simón Vélez

Club Puerto Peñalisa.
Detail of the structure
of the main building.
One can see the iron
fittings that join the
guaduas to the roof
and which have
cement mortar injected
into the internodes,
a technique which
makes possible these
enormous cantilever
roofs.
Ricaurte,
Cundinamarca,
Colombia.

Here we see the
kind of crane that is
characteristic of big
construction projects.
The social center of
this golf club is still
the biggest guadua
structure designed
by Simón Vélez, with
a roof area of 2,200
square meters.
Ricaurte,
Cundinamarca,
Colombia.

Puerto Peñalisa Club.
This was the first time
that a major
Colombian
construction firm,
Mazuera y Cia,
employed guadua
as the basic element
of a large project.
Ricaurte,
Cundinamarca,
Colombia.

Main social center.
Puerto Peñalisa.
Ricaurte,
Cundinamarca,
Colombia.

Detail of roof, main
social center, with its
framework of guadua
in "par y nudillo."
Puerto Peñalisa.
Ricaurte,
Cundinamarca,
Colombia.

Kiosk for
social activities.
Puerto Peñalisa.
Ricaurte,
Cundinamarca,
Colombia.

Kiosk.
A small, two-story
octagonal pavilion.
A mixed construction
of concrete, boulders,
steel and wood, with
a roof structure of
guadua and ceramic
tiles.
Puerto Peñalisa.
Ricaurte,
Cundinamarca,
Colombia.

Covered horse trough.
Puerto Peñalisa.
Ricaurte,
Cundinamarca,
Colombia.

Porter's Lodge.
Puerto Peñalisa.
Ricaurte,
Cundinamarca,
Colombia.

Detail of the roof and living room of the country house. Puerto Peñalisa. Ricaurte, Cundinamarca, Colombia.

Country house.
Puerto Peñalisa.
Ricaurte,
Cundinamarca,
Colombia.

Pages 80/81
Following pages,
Cupula in guadua
and *macana* (see p.
82) for a house in a
cool climate.
Bogotá, Colombia.

Cupolas in guadua and *macana* for a country house on the eastern ridges that overlook Bogotá. *Macana* is the outer fiber, very strong and resistant, of most palms. The bows and arrows of the indigenous people were often fabricated out of this material. In the coffee zone it is typically used for verandah banisters and window lattices. La Calera, Cundinamarca, Colombia.

*Opposite page
and above*
Mezzanine with
cantilever bed for
the siesta, utilizing
guaduas with their
roots.
Quinta Galería.
Bogotá, Colombia.

Pages 86-87
Casa Alejandro
Martínez.
Built in a very cold
climate at more than
3,000 meters above
sea level. You can
see the cupola of
the living room which

faces the landscape
and the opposite end,
with the intersections
of the cupolas of the
bedrooms.
Sesquilé,
Cundinamarca,
Colombia.

Pages 88-89
Details of two
cupolas.
Bogotá, Colombia.

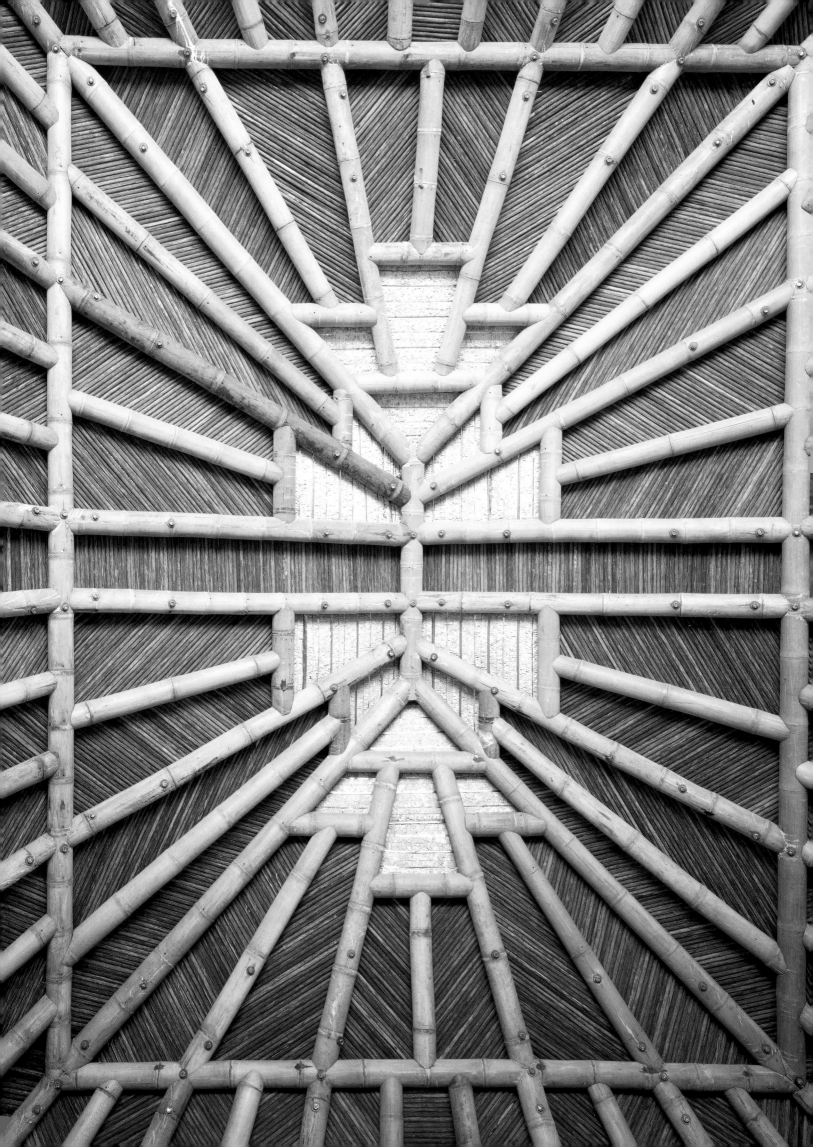

Loft bedroom and detail
of cupola in the
bedroom with mezzanine.
Tabio, Cundinamarca,
Colombia.

Opposite page
Pottery Studio
More than thirty
structures of the "par y
nudillo" type have

been built by this
architect for different
purposes.
Tabio, Cundinamarca,
Colombia.

Milking-shed for cows. Structure built after visiting the island of Bali in Indonesia, where there is a rich and beautiful tradition of using bamboo. Tenjo, Cundinamarca, Colombia.

Opposite page
The "Plantamos"
greenhouse is a
building with a steel
structure and a glass
roof and walls. Its
interior is lined with a
row of *chusque*
bamboo that provides
shade to protect the
plants from the intense
solar radiation of
Bogotá.

The *chusque* is a stout
bamboo with a small
diameter that grows at
2,200 meters above
sea level or higher
and in Spanish colonial
times was the most
commonly-used material
for the ceilings of the
roofs of dwellings in
the Andean high
savanna around Bogotá.
Bogotá, Colombia.

Above
The "Jaibaná" nursery
is a "par y nudillo"
structure, characteristic
of roof structures
during the Spanish
colonial period and
also found in most
of the roof structures
designed by Simón

Vélez. It reaches an
interior span of 13
meters, with a
cantilever roof of 6
meters on each side.
Fusagasugá,
Cundinamarca,
Colombia.

Pages 96/97
Descafecol
Manizales, Caldas,
Colombia.

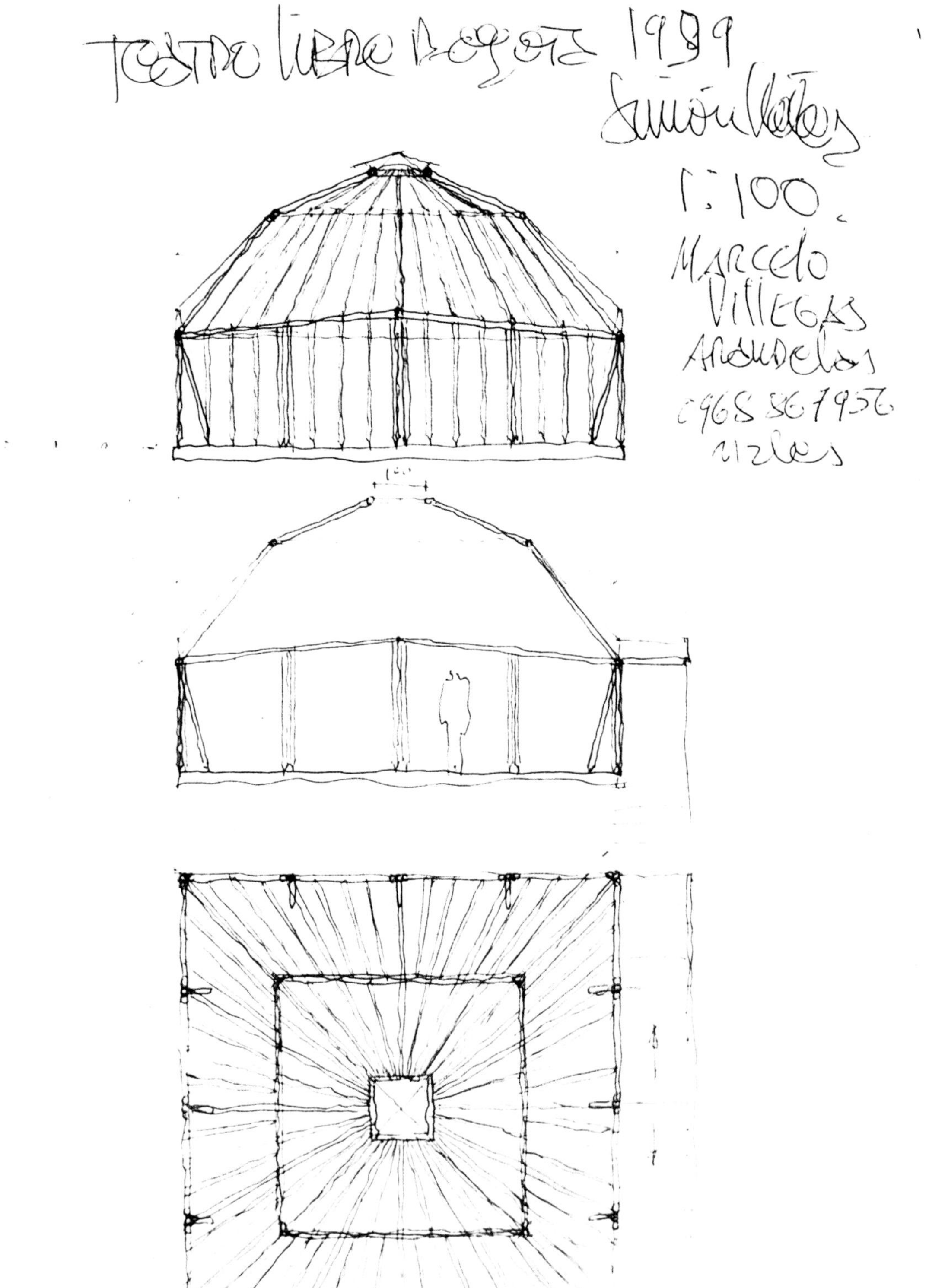

TEATRO LIBRE BOGOTÁ 1989
Simón Vélez
1:100
MARCELO
VILLEGAS
ARQUITECTOS
0965 80 1952
cielos

Rehearsal hall of
the Teatro Libre of
Bogotá, without
windows and with
overhead illumination
and ventilation, in
a guadua structure.
Bogotá, Colombia.

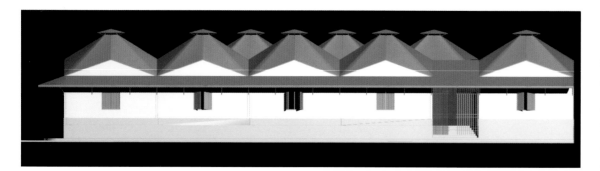

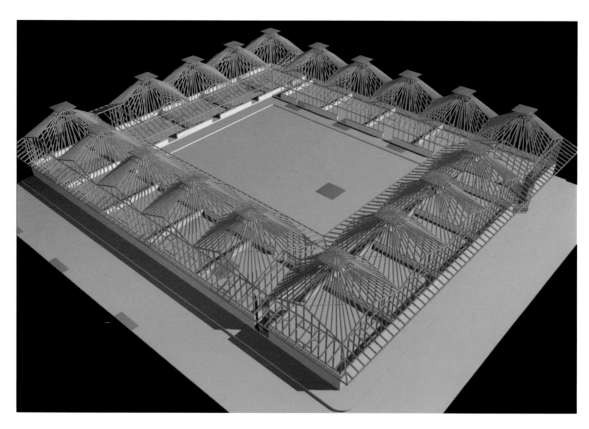

In February, 1999 an earthquake hit the Colombian coffee zone, leaving thousands of children without schools. In Barcelona, Quindío, a number of institutions and persons were invited to a meeting sponsored by UNICEF, among them, the famous Spanish singer-composer Joan Manuel Serrat and Simón Vélez, who made the main contributions for the realization of this work, which has roofs with a structure of guadua.

Left
Computer mock-ups of the project.

Barcelona School
Barcelona, Quindío,
Colombia.

Above
Living room of a house
in the historic part of
Bogotá, with a cupola
built of guadua, chairs

made of guadua roots
by Marcelo Villegas
and columns of
mangrove bundles.
Floors in *sapán* wood.

Opposite page
Main bedroom of the
same house, with a
view over the historic
sector of Bogotá, built
of very slender
guaduas.
Bogotá, Colombia.

Casa Jorge Rocha, near Bogotá, with pavilion, social area and pool. The corner pillars are of masonry, the central columns are of *guayacán* logs, the tie-beam is concrete and the roof structure in guadua supports the tile roof. Bannisters of *macana*. Cundinamarca, Colombia.

Inspired by the farmhouses of the coffee belt, this house with a L-shaped floor plan has peripheral corridors on its two floors. Mixed construction of stone, concrete, iron and *guayacán* and *costillo* logs. The *chusque* bamboo seen above the corridor serves as a form for the second floor. Tiled roof over a guadua framework. Fusagasugá, Cundinamarca, Colombia.

One of the 15 proposals for housing submitted to "Café de Colombia", the national coffee-growers federation, with the aim of giving growers affected by the 1999 earthquake in the coffee zone the opportunity to choose the one they most liked. No one chose this house. In Colombia, guadua still suffers the stigma of being associated with poverty and only the wealthier classes are beginning to appreciate it as a positive and beautiful construction material. The same prototype was constructed in France in 1999 as a practical exercise in the POMPIDOU-VITRA workshop and was granted a construction license in that country.

Prototype of a low-cost
peasant-farmer
dwelling.
La "Y". Quindio,
Colombia.

Prototype of a low-cost
peasant-farmer
dwelling in Cerritos,
Risaralda, Colombia.

Lookout Tower
Parque del Café
(The Coffee Park).
Quindío, Colombia.
Designed by Simón
Vélez and Marcelo
Villegas.

Guadua scaffolding
used during
construction.

Structure of log
columns made of
bunches of mangrove
which stand on cast
steel joints set in the
concrete foundation.
Stairways, banisters,
terminal columns and
floor of the tower in
abarco wood. 19
meters-high roof with a
structure of guadua,
covered by ceramic
tiles.

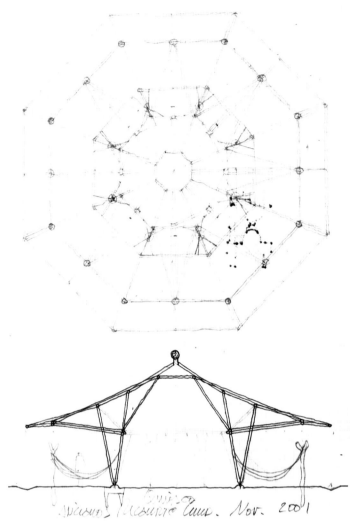

Kiosk for an old
people´s home
A very demanding
structure because of
the slenderness of
its guadua columns,
which support a heavy
roof of mortar and
ceramic tiles. Where
the columns reach
the floor they are
supported by a
number of cast bronze
balls anchored in the
concrete foundation.
Observe, on the
right, the detail of
the traction ring of the
roof, made of rebars
and guadua.
Ricaurte,
Cundinamarca,
Colombia.

Above
San Jorge Kiosk
Pereira, Risaralda,
Colombia

Below and opposite page
"Constructora Melendez" Kiosk. Octagonal structure supported by bunches of mangrove slightly inclined towards the interior. It stands in the middle of an artificial lake raised four feet above ground level by artificial embankments. One enters by passing through a services building to a concrete walkway at water level. The roof has a guadua structure. Cali, Valle del Cauca, Colombia.

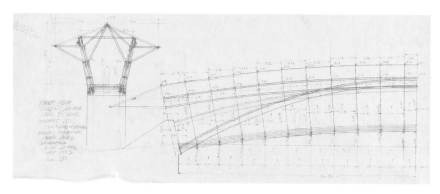

Jenny Garzón Bridge
Joint project: Bogotá
Institute of Urban
Development, Sena
(National
Apprenticeship
Service) and Bambú
de Colombia

Covered bridge
with a tubular structure
of guadua arches.
45.6 meters span
2.5 meters wide
walkway made of
a 10 centimeter-thick
cement slab weighing
30 tons.
Roof area of 500
square meters,
made of Spanish-type
ceramic tiles resting
on cement mortar,
with a weight of
250 kilograms/square
meter or a total
weight of 125 tons.
Load bearing
capacity: 45 tons.

Hacienda house
Pereira, Risaralda,
Colombia.

"*Paloca*": the name is a combination of the words for two traditional thatched-roof structures, the "Palapa" of Mexico, and the "Maloca", the indigenous long-house of the Colombian Amazon. Columns in *costillo*-wood which start and end in ball and socket joints of cast bronze, so that they touch neither the upper structure of guadua nor the stones of the floor. Zicaru Huatulco, Oaxaca, México. Design by Carlos Herrera, Jorge Herrera and Simón Vélez.

In southern Mexico, in the states of Tabasco and Chiapas, the entrepreneur Alfonso Romo planted more than 1,000 hectares of *Guadua angustifolia*. The plantlets of guadua were brought from Colombia, along with an agronomist who is a specialist in their reproduction, Homilson Cruz. The biggest single plantation in Colombia does not surpass 100 hectares: this gives an idea of the dimension of Mexico's potential for this resource. This is also the first structure built in Mexico of guadua imported from Colombia. Zicaru Hautulco, Oaxaca, Mexico Designed by Carlos Herrera, Jorge Herrera and Simón Vélez.

Stage, "Island Village", the cultural center dedicated to Jamaican music. Octagonal roof supported by four groups of columns, each made up of three posts of Canadian pine, joined by cups of cast bronze. The guadua structure is also joined to the floor columns. In the upper detail, observe the traction ring and stainless steel rods, connected to the guaduas by means of cement mortar injected into their hollow internodes. This is the first guadua structure built in the Caribbean and may mark the start of a culture of guadua-use in Jamaica, where bamboo (*bambusa vulgaris*) is found throughout the island. Ocho Ríos, Jamaica. Designed by Ann Hodges and Simón Vélez.

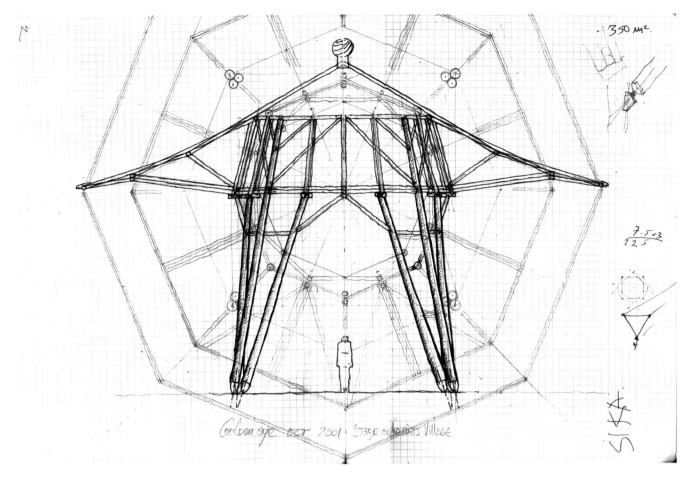

Carloon eye oct 2001 · Stage ochos rios Village

350 m².

$\frac{7.5+3}{12.5}$

SIKA

The Rotunda.
Entrance to the cultural
center dedicated to
Jamaican music.
Guadua was used for
the roof structure and
Canadian pine for the
columns.
Ocho Ríos, Jamaica.
Designed by
Ann Hodges
and Simón Vélez.

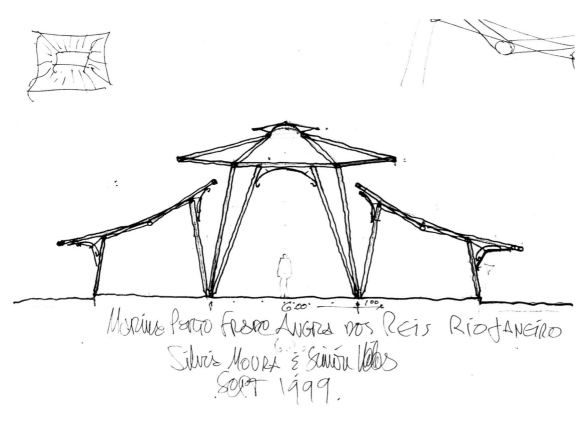

Marina Porto Frade Angra dos Reis Rio Janeiro
Silvio Moura & Simón Velez
Sept 1999.

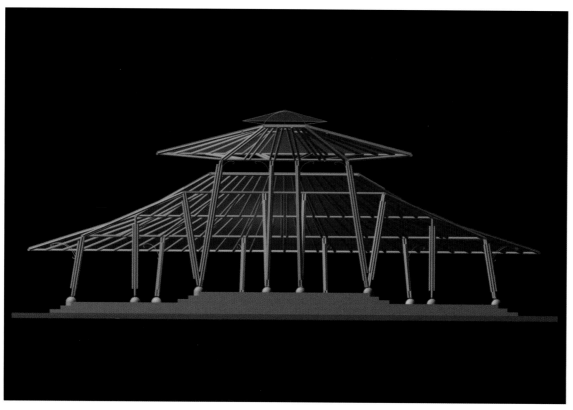

Hotel do Frade,
Restaurant.
Structure made with
*Dendrocalamus
gigante*, an Asian
tropical bamboo
brought to Brazil by
the Portuguese. Brazil
harbors more square
kilometers of different
species of guadua
than any other country
in the world.
Angra dos Reis.
Río de Janeiro, Brazil
Designed by Silvia
Moura, Elio Pellegrino
and Simón Vélez.

Hotel do Frade,
Restaurant.
This structure, built in
the year 2000, may
also become the start
of a guadua culture in
that enormous country.
In contrast with
Colombia, where the
popular use of guadua
has traditionally been
a symbol of poverty,
there are no
prejudices against this
material in Brazil,
which means that
there is a very
promising future for
guadua buildings
there.
Angra dos Reis.
Río de Janeiro, Brazil
Designed by Silvia
Moura, Elio Pellegrino
and Simón Vélez.

Liquid Jungle Lab.
Central America.
Detail of roof with
"chicken foot"
structure.
Design: Marco Zanini.
Consultant for
engineering aspects of
the guadua roof:
Simón Vélez.

129

Detail of finishing at
the corner of the main
corridor, next to the
dining room. The
columns of logs bear
the weight of a very
heavy roof. Only very
fine timber is capable
of resisting these
stresses.

Opposite page
Community building.
Central America.
Under construction,
2002.
Design: Simón Vélez
Interior design:
Marco Zanini.
Sottsass Associados.

Biology laboratory.
Central America.
Under construction,
2000.
Sottsass Asociados
Engineering design for
the guadua roof:
Simón Vélez.

Main house
Central America.
Under construction,
2002.
Design: Simón Vélez
Interior design:
Marco Zanini
Sottsass Associados

Above
Detail of main
bedroom. "Par y
nudillo" roof structure,

Below
Detail of the roof of
the main bedroom,
under construction.
Cantiliver roofs with a
7.6 meters span.
Bundles of guadua
joined to the concrete
with cast bronze cups.

Above
Detail of the roof of
the main bedroom.

Below
Detail of the roof
of the kitchen of the
main house.

Plastic half-bottles of "S. Pellegrino" mineral water, filled with cement mortar, serve as the tips of the guadua columns, under the principle of "Protection through design".

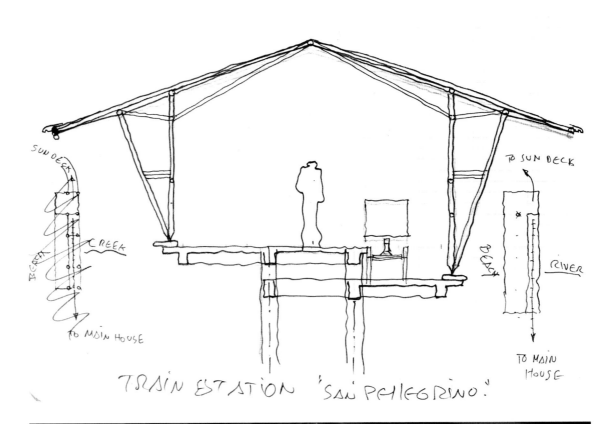

TRAIN ESTATION 'SAN PELEGRINO'

Train station
Central America.
This structure is
inspired in the
structure of a brick
works near Manizales,
Colombia.

Guest House
Bahía Honda,
Central America

Construction techniques
as an expression of
tropical diversity and
the extraordinary crafts
skills of the workers.
The reference which
served as the starting
point for the design of
this house with a two-
slope roof may be seen
in the coffee drying.

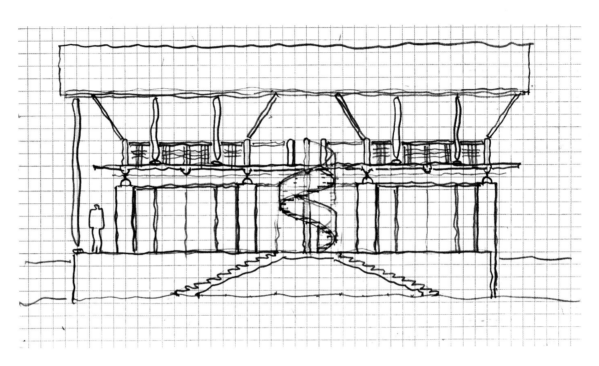

Second storey, whose center rests on concrete columns fastened to the concrete slab by cast bronze washers. The exterior columns of logs, which are very hard, also use bronze washers to support the slab of the second floor. The form for the concrete second floor was made with diagonally-placed guaduas that support a *macana* ceiling with a fishbone pattern which bears the massive weight of the concrete.

Together with the Centre Georges Pompidou, Paris, and the C. I. R. E. C. A. (Centre International de Recherche et d'Education Culturelle et Agricole; International Center for Cultural and Agricultural Research and Education), the Vitra Design Museum has offered interdisciplinary summer workshops for the last six years in the Domaine de Boisbuchet, a historical country estate in southwest France. The seminars are focussed on practical work. The mock-ups show 4 different exercises in guadua structures, corresponding to the 4 summer workshops taught by Simón Vélez, in 1998, 1999, 2000 and 2001. In 1999 the workshop was devoted to the peasant-farmer house (see page 106-107) proposed for the coffee zone of Colombia after the earthquake of that year. This house and constructional technique obtained a building license in France.

Alexander von Vegesack, director of the Vitra Museum; Jean Detheir, consultant architect of the Georges Pompidou Center; Simón Vélez; the Moroccan architect Elie Mouyal; and Shigeru Ban, the Japanese architect who designed the Japan Pavilion in Expo-Hannover 2000 (pages 62-63).

Workshop-Seminars in
La Domaine de
Boisbuchet France.

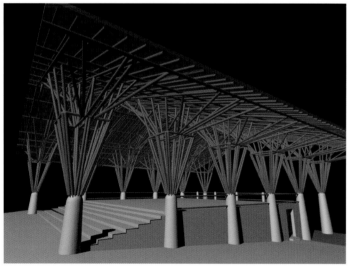

Above, right and left
A design, never
executed, for a school
of circus arts,
intended to provide
an educational
alternative for young
people who live in the
poor districts of Cali.
Cali, Valle del Cauca,
Colombia.

Below, right and left
Project for an
auditorium that has not
yet been constructed.
James Bond Beach.
Oracabeza, Jamaica.
Designed by
Ann Hodges
and Simón Vélez.

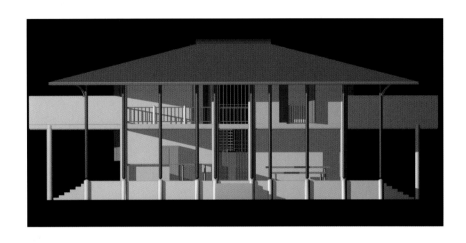

Above and center
Computer mock-up for coffee-plantation house, with a square floor plan. The two storey-high corridor running round the house resembles that of the plantation mansions of the ante-bellum South.

Below
Mock-up of a guadua pavilion to house exhibitions of bamboo-crafts. Project ordered by the Mayor's Office of Paris, France.

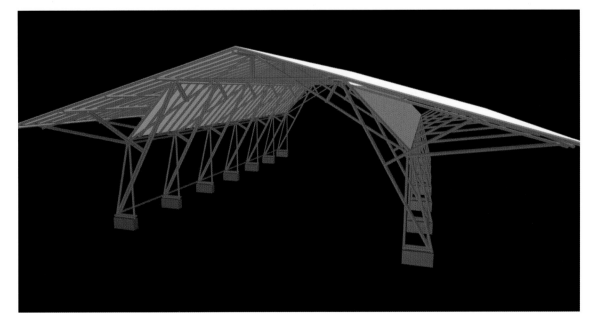

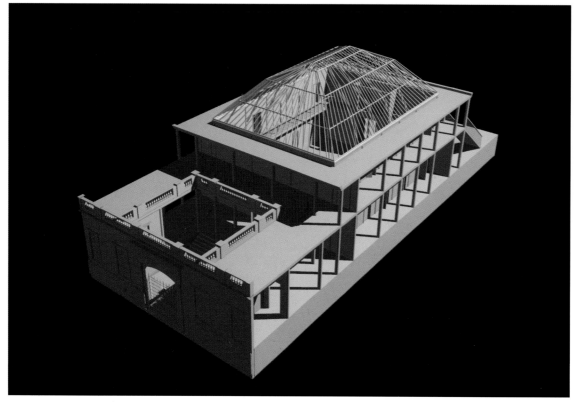

Virtual mock-up of the rehearsal hall for young musicians of the Batuta Foundation. The National Monuments office denied building permission for this project in guadua, on the grounds that it would interfere with the historic sector of Bogotá for which it was planned. In Colombia, architects' prejudices against guadua are nearly insuperable. Bogotá, Colombia.

Above
Mock-up of project for the "Torre de Chipre", unbuilt, with a structure of wood and guadua and a roof with a guadua base Lago de Aranguito. Manizales, Caldas, Colombia. 1996

Below
Virtual mock-ups of the project for the Lookout Tower of the "Parque del Café" – The Coffee Park –, still to be built, with a structure of wood and guadua and a roof with a guadua base. Pereira, Risaralda, Colombia. 2000

Page 146
Studio of Marcelo Villegas. Manizales, Caldas, Colombia.

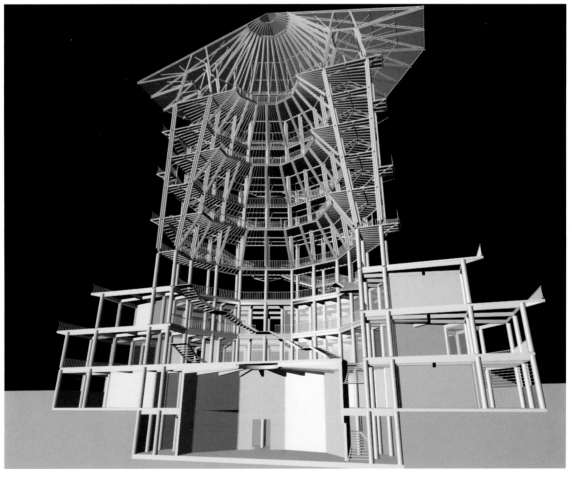

Marcelo Villegas

"The tradition of arts and crafts that disappeared with the advent of what is wrongly known as modern architecture and the industrialized mass consumption of the objects of everyday life like furniture and utensils was reborn in this studio, in which, with all the integrity of the artisan, guadua, wood, cast iron, leather, machinery, mechanics, and alchemy come to life in the hands of Marcelo Villegas and his workers."

Simón Vélez

Studio of Marcelo Villegas, with chair made of guadua roots.
Manizales, Caldas, Colombia.

148

Detail of bend in the "par y nudillo" roof of the studio. Manizales, Caldas, Colombia.

Detail of the studio of Marcelo Villegas, with a structure in carved *nato*-wood. Manizales, Caldas, Colombia.

Opposite page
Studio of Marcelo Villegas.
Table and bench in *caoba*-wood, guadua roots as legs and cast iron tips.
Manizales, Caldas, Colombia.

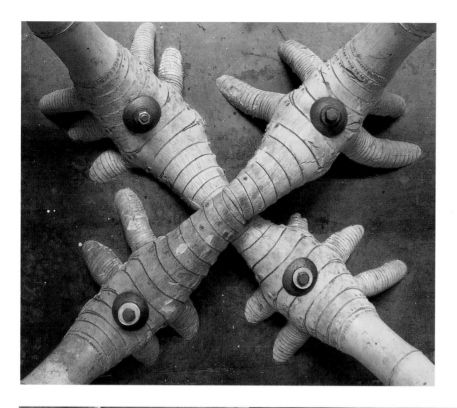

Guadua rhizomes
intercrossed to form
bases for tables,
anchored to steel
plates with forged
fittings.

Drawing and structure
of a two-seat sofa,
assembled from
guadua rhizomes.

Armchair "Model 48".
Made of guadua
rhizomes, with a
curved block of *nato*-
wood as the back and
seat of saddle leather.

"Partnership"
Armchair, ("Silla en
compañía"), so-called
because it was jointly
designed by Marcelo
Villegas and Simón
Vélez. Front legs of
22 cm-diameter
guaduas. Armrests in
sapán-wood. Back and
seat in saddle leather.

Table and bench in
caoba-wood and
macana, with legs of
guadua rhizomes.
Galería Cano Bavaria
Bogotá, Colombia.

Opposite page
Table (with the design
drawings). Top In
caoba-wood and
macana. Legs of
guadua rhizomes.
Galería Cano Bavaria
Bogotá, Colombia.

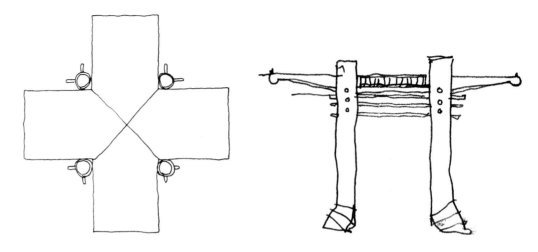

Sheik´s chair
With back and seat
made of two tabular
roots of *nato*-wood.
Legs made of guadua
rhizomes.

Double-curve
armchair.
Assembled from eight
guadua rhizomes, with
seat in saddle leather.
Fittings of cast bronze.

Opposite page
Horseshoe armchair.
Assembled from ten
guadua rhizomes.
Seat in saddle leather.

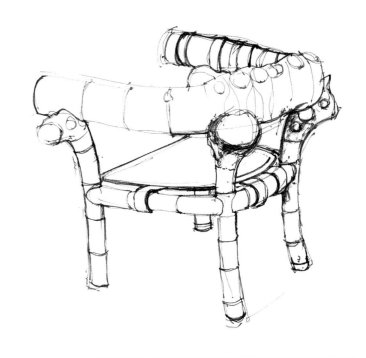

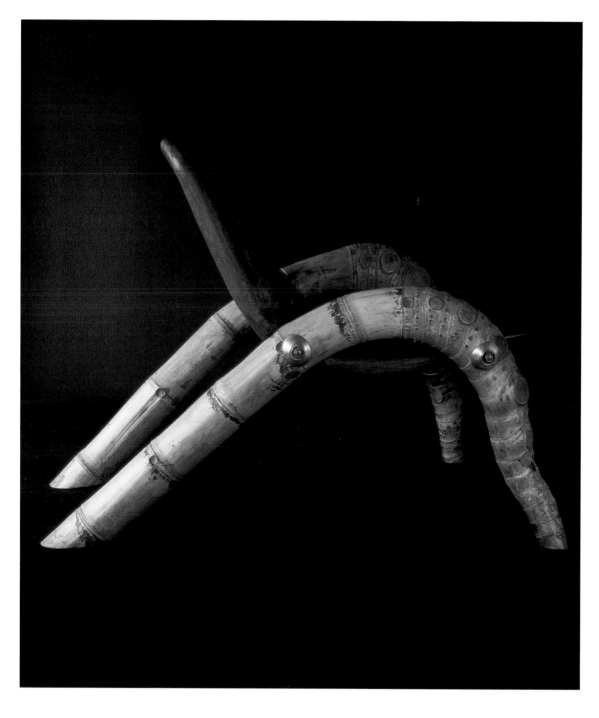

Chairs made of "bamba", that is, the tabular root of *nato*-wood. They make use of the root's natural shape for the back and seat, which are worked so as to achieve the correct ergometrics. They rest on arched guadua roots and have fittings of cast bronze.

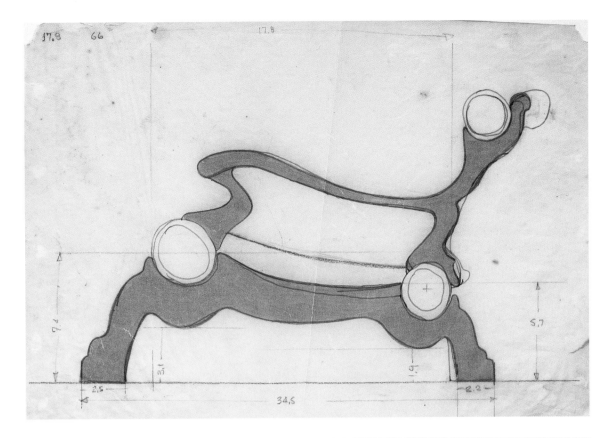

Sofa (with design
drawing). *Caoba,*
sapán and guadua.

"Scissors" chair, assembled from two pieces of the tabular roots of *nato*-wood, with guadua-rhizome legs.

Opposite page, above
Table with legs of rhizomes, anchored to a metallic base and a top made from a single block of the tabular root of *nato*.

Opposite page, below
Table with guadua-rhizome legs ending in cast iron tips and a top made from a single block of the tabular root of *nato*.

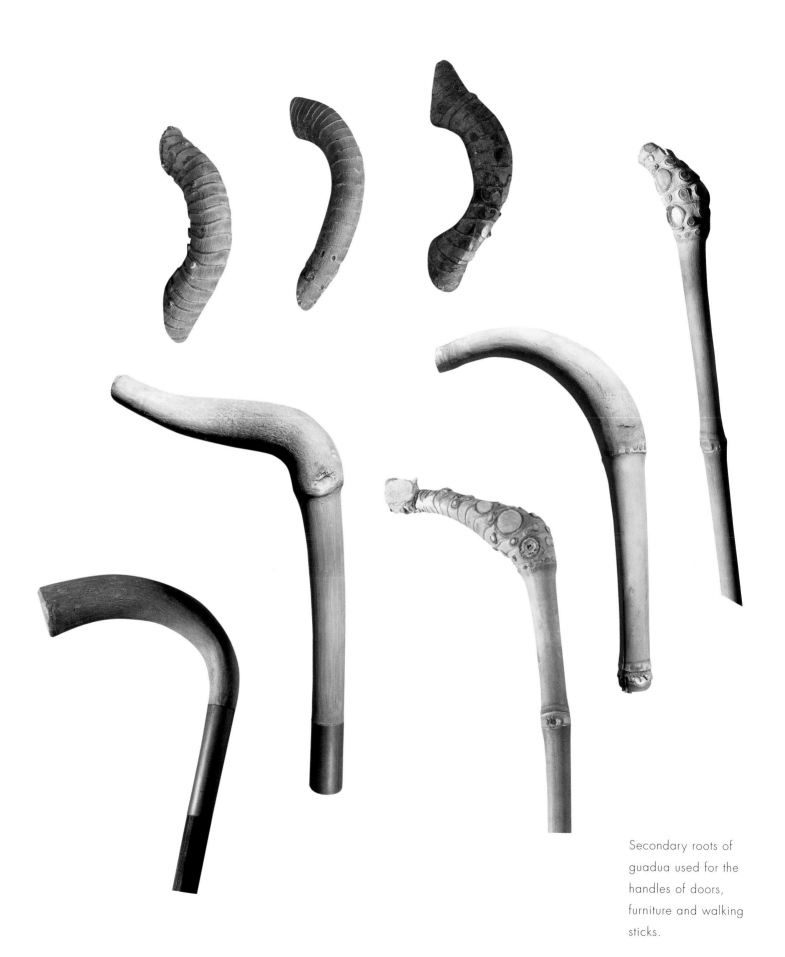

Secondary roots of guadua used for the handles of doors, furniture and walking sticks.

Coat and hat racks
made from guadua
rhizomes.

Handrail for a
stairway made of a
single piece of
guadua with its root.
Galería Cano.
Bogotá, Colombia.

Console table with top made of a tabular root of *nato*-wood upheld by a "hand" of guadua.

Cedar wood table and wooden benches with legs made of guadua rhizomes that end in metal tips.

Round container with detachable top, made of turned guadua.

Containers of guadua with a top of *cedro macho*–wood and *congolo* handle.

Copper ashtrays with guadua base.

Opposite page
Files and adzes with handles made of guadua root.

Structure for
greenhouses for fruit
or garden produce.
10 meter-long
guaduas are anchored
in the ground and bent
to produce a span of
8 meters. It is the
cheapest and quickest
building alternative.
Santágueda, Caldas,
Colombia

Left
Hacienda El Paso.
Tower of the guest
pavilion.

Below
"par y nudillo" roof
of the studio of the
painter Jenaro Mejía.

Hacienda El Paso.
Services pavilion.
Mixed construction.
Masonry walls.
Main columns in
carved *nato*-wood.
Guadua in the roof
structures.
Pereira, Risaralda,
Colombia.

Guadalupe
Santágueda, Caldas,
Colombia.

Opposite page
Detail of compression
ring in the octagonal
roof with a ten meters
diameter.

Above
Main front of the two-
story hacienda house.

Left
Detail of the estate
manager´s house.

177

Media Torta open-air concert hall in Chipre.

Open-air concert hall in Manizales. Caldas, Colombia.

A roof that follows the slope in order to take advantage of the view from Manizales towards the river Cauca.

Parasol structure. Wooden columns with "protection through design" in the base. Santágueda, Caldas, Colombia.

Casa Diablos
Santágueda, Caldas,
Colombia.

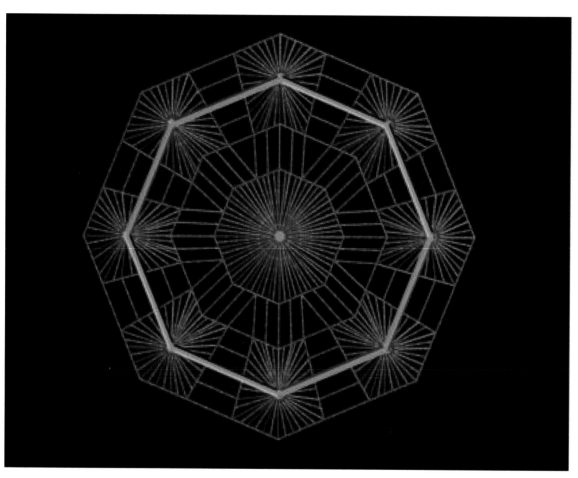

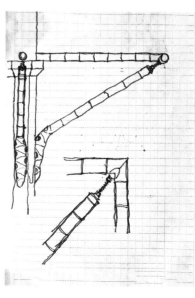

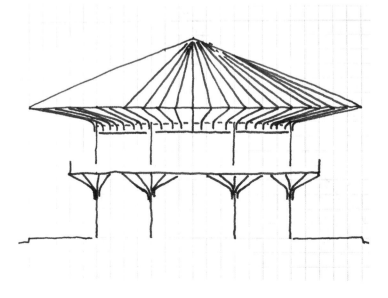

Left and opposite page
Project for the country
seat of the Once
Caldas soccer club.
Caldas, Colombia.
2000
Post-stressed system for
the foundation of the
second storey.

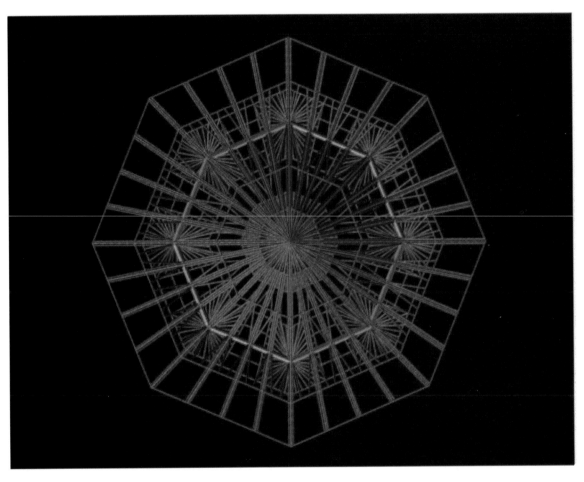

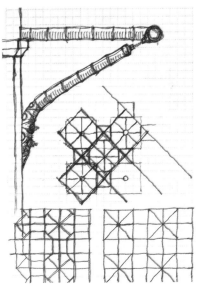

Page 184
Lamps
Designed by Lucas
Jaramillo
Bogotá, Colombia.

Pages 186/187
Lamps
Juan Manuel Esguerra
and Ricardo Quiroga.
Laboratorio
Colombiano de
Diseño, Armenia,
Colombia.
Artesanías de
Colombia. Bogotá.

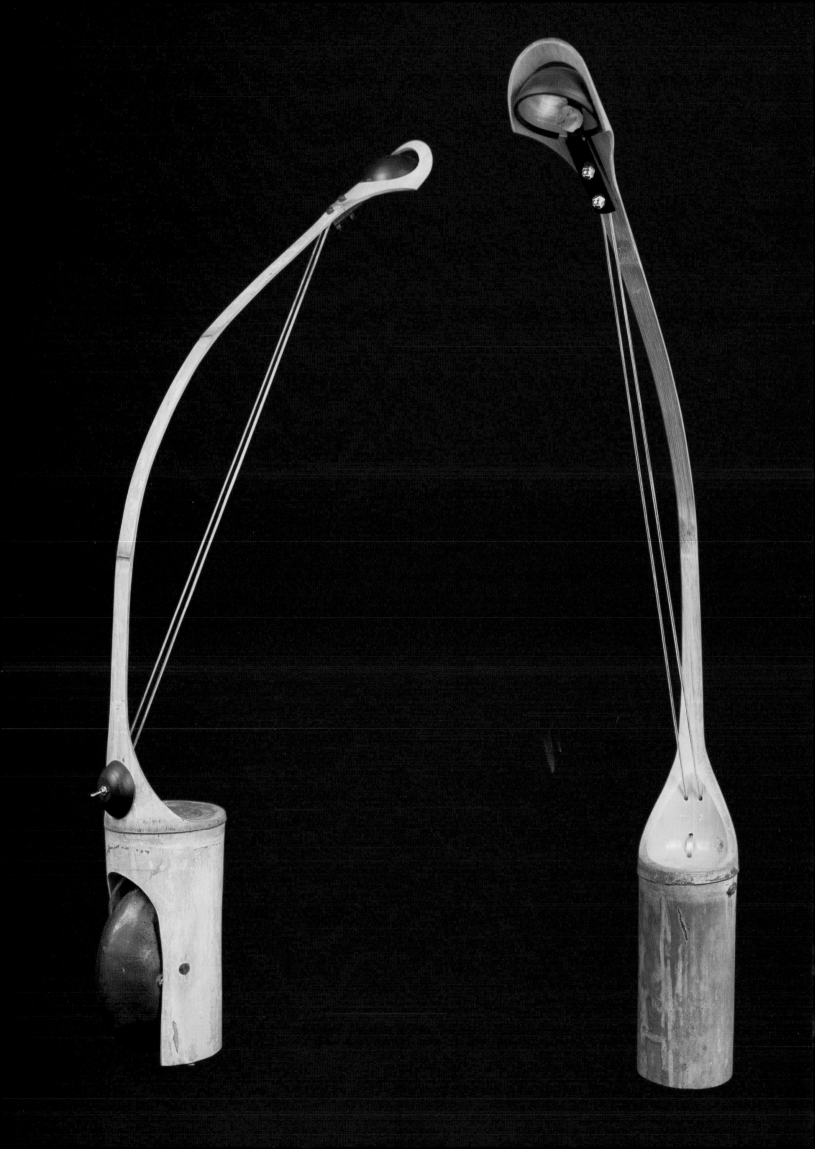

LUCAS JARAMILLO

JUAN MANUEL ESGUERRA

RICARDO QUIROGA

ALEJANDRO CABO

GABRIEL GERMÁN LONDOÑO

GILBERTO JARAMILLO

VICTORIA PETERS

JULIANA GÓMEZ

ARTURO AGUIRRE

OLGA TROCONIS

RODRIGO FERNÁNDEZ

GOTZ SCHMITT

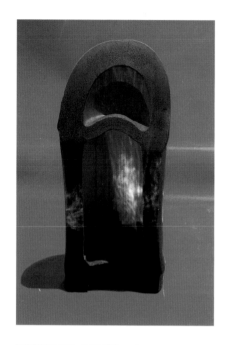

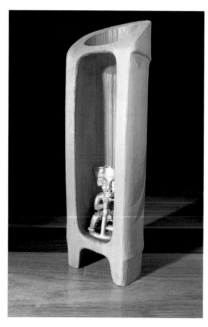

The Fracture of the Solar Disc. Construction – Dseconstruction. "Guadua as a concave-convex element, a receptacle that contains a void with a psycho-spiritual magic for multiple mental associations. In this exhibition of pre-Columbian pieces, our culture (lost or hidden) is associated with our inner space, that is to say, with the house of the soul.

In opposition to the above, a geometrized cubic structure that has distanced us from nature oppresses us in our passions: the defense of property with anger; love with lust; the vanity of belief without knowledge, without a correct questioning; an enormous desire for profit; a devotion to every kind of cultural cleverness and methods of improper conduct that specifically lead to the destruction of ourselves and of nature. A reflection that may allow us to think about a new design, for a new image of life more in harmony with nature. To use bamboo as a symbol for a new industrial revolution."

Alejandro Cabo

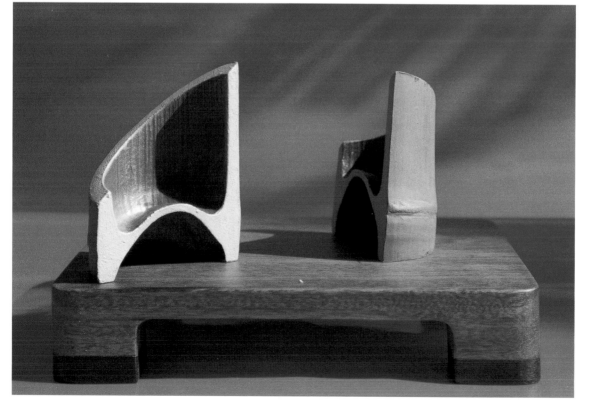

Stands for gold artifacts. Designed by Alejandro Cabo Bogotá, Colombia.

188

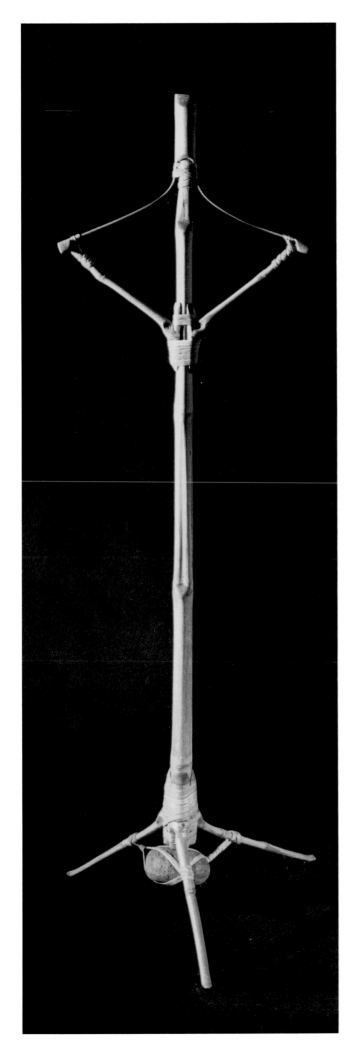

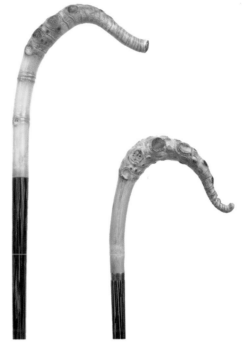

Walking sticks and
display case for
butterflies.
Designed by Gabriel
Germán Londoño
Pereira, Colombia.

Hat and coat rack and
lectern.
Designed by Gilberto
Jaramillo
Taller Cantarrana
Neira, Colombia.

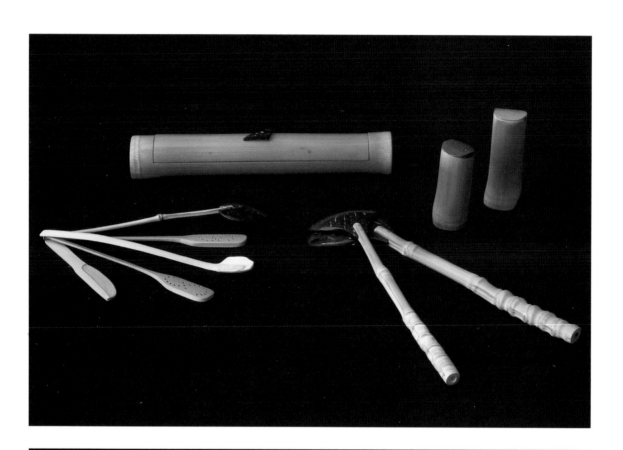

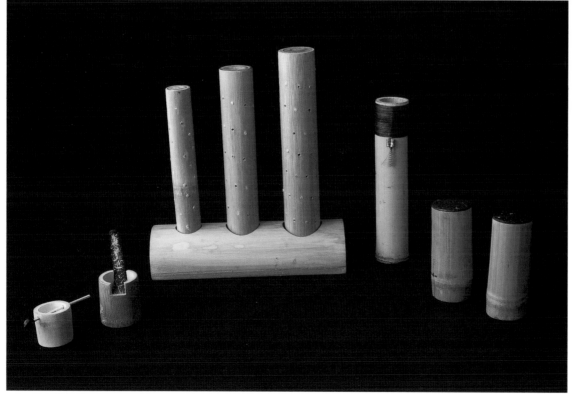

Above
Kaleidoscope and
saltcellars.
Designed by Victoria
Peters.
Rain sticks.
Designed by Juliana
Gómez.

Below
Saltcellar and pepper
pot in guadua and
coconut shell top.
Saltcellar with coconut
spoon. Bambú diseños
DEK
Bogotá, Colombia.

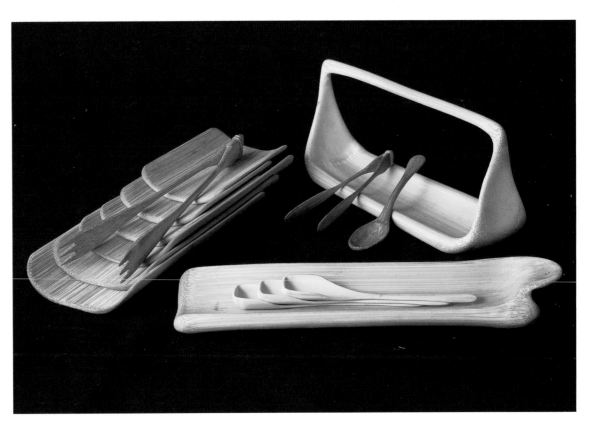

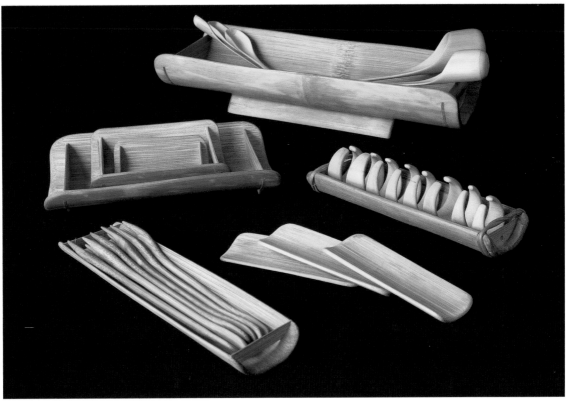

Above
Plates, baskets, salad
server and spoons.
Gauba.
Design: Victoria
Peters.
Proyecta.
Bogotá, Colombia.

Below
Plates, napkin holders,
spoons and forks.
Manos talladoras
Designed by Arturo
Aguirre and Olga
Troconis.
Tabio, Cundinamarca,
Colombia.

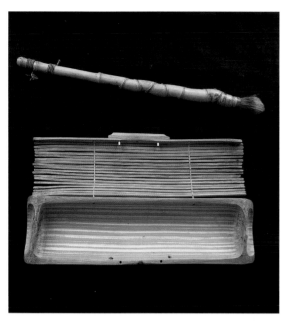

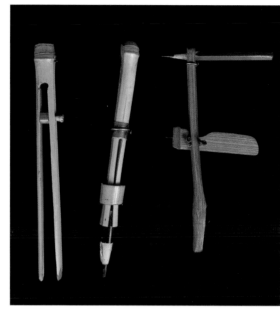

Above
Paintbrush and box.
Tweezers, pencil
holder and compass.

Below
Rattle, sticks for
reading the *I Ching*
and book marks
Design Rodrigo
Fernández.
Bogotá, Colombia.

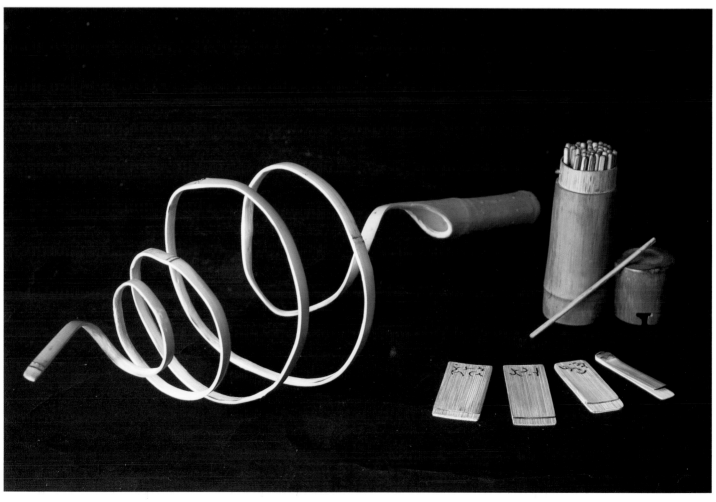

This organ, which has 60 pipes made of guadua cane out of a total of 840, may be unique. It was built by the German priests Jorge Bauer and Patricio Fassnacht in the monastery of the Benedictine Fathers in El Rosal, Cundinamarca, with the help and advice of Óscar Winder, a famous German organ builder. The organ parts, made in Germany, reached Colombia in 1978. Some of the pipes, which came from distant European monasteries, date back to 1840 and 1878. The keyboard, which belonged to an organ in an old German abbey, was built in 1905.

Industrial uses of guadua

GÖTZ SCHMITT

"For centuries bamboo has been used in everyday life in many different cultures throughout the world. This user-friendly 'grass' is employed for a multitude of things, including musical instruments, furniture and houses. The reason: no other natural resource possesses more elasticity, hardness and strength. Since ancient times the people of the Orient have regarded bamboo as a symbol of flexibility and strength.

Bamboo produces four times more wood than, for example, oak. Whenever we use bamboo we make a valuable contribution to the environment, since we leave the much slower growing hardwood forests untouched.

Bamboo produces substantially more oxygen than trees and therefore plays a vital role in a healthy eco-system. It also prevents soil erosion due to the extensive clumping of its root system.

As a building material, bamboo can easily withstand a comparison with wood. The fibres of bamboo are up to 1cm long, while those of wood are only 2mm long, approximately. Bamboo possesses only a small proportion of lignin. Its main component is silicic acid, which gives the shoot its durability and hardness.

For the past 10 years, with the help of other bamboo fanatics, I have been discovering the beauty and multiple uses of the high technology material, made by Mother Earth, which is called bamboo/guadua.

So far as I can judge, the widespread use of bamboo is on the point of a breakthrough. We already supply bamboo products to more than 20 countries. They include flooring, boards, a veneer that may be as thin as 0.2 mm , and bamboo fibre for the garment and automotive industries.

Bamboo is becoming a material that replaces wood, with the advantage of a faster growth and a greater versatility. The exploitation of bamboo material may soon reach 100%. For example, we now produce a barbecue grill charcoal made out of bamboo. Our aim is a material that produces zero emissions and this goal has already been achieved.

In short, I see a great future for bamboo and for the people who work and live with bamboo. It can create income and overcome social problems and poverty, especially in the rural areas of many countries around the equator".

Interior design, furniture and conference hall realized by the "Elephant" firm of Germany. Elephant is the market's leading supplier of bamboo goods, with an exclusive technology that even allows it to provide the automobile industry with bamboo components for "green", that is, environmentally-friendly cars.

Index of photographs

Bibliography

CASTAÑO, F. 1993. *La silvicultura de la guadua en Colombia*. Pp. 69-72 *in* Memorias del Primer Congreso Mundial del Bambu/Guadua, Pereira, Colombia, 8-15 Agosto 1992. Servicio Nacional de Aprendizaje, Bogotá.

CLARK, L.G. 1993. *Diversity and distribution of the Andean woody bamboos (Poaceae: Bambuseae)*. Symposia "The Andean Montaine Forest", The New York Botanical Garden, June 1993.

CLARK, L.G. 1990. *Diversity and biogeography of Neotropical bamboos (Poaceae: Bambusoideae)*. Acta Botánica Brasílica 4:125-132.

CLARK, L.G., W. ZHANG AND J. F. WENDEL. 1995. *A phylogeny of the grass family (Poaceae) based on ndhF sequence data*. Systematic Botany 20:436-460.

DAGILIS, T.D., & Turcke, D.J. 1996. "An Economical Bamboo Particleboard", Bamboo, People and the Environment, Volume 3: Engineering and Utilization. (The proceedings of the IV International Bamboo Congress, Bali, Indonesia, held June 1995), International Development Bamboo Centre (IDRC).

GIECC, 1996. Climate change 1995. Contribution of WGI to the second assessment report of the IPCC. Cambridge University Press.

GIRALDO, E., & A. SABOGAL. 1999. *Una alternativa sostenible: La Guadua*. Corporación Autónoma Regional del Quindío C.R.Q, 192 pp.

GNANAHARAN, R., J.J.A. JANSEEN and O. ARCE, 1994. *Bending Strength of* Guadua *Bamboo*. Comparison of Different Testing Procedures. 24 pp. INBAR Working Paper No. 3. New Delhi, India.

JIAFU, L. 2000. The development strategy of bamboo resource and bamboo industry in China, *in* International training workshop on sustainable bamboo management and processing techniques for small-size bamboo enterprises, Hangzhou, China, Oct. 4-16, Pg. 1-21.

JUDZIEWICZ, E., L.G. CLARK, X. LONDOÑO, & M. J. STERN. 1999. American bamboos. Smithsonian Institution Press, Washington & Londono, 392 pp.

LATIF, M. AND LIESE, W., 2001. Anatomical features of *Bambusa vulgaris* and *Gigantochloa scortechinii* from four harvesting sites in Peninsular Malaysia. Journal of Tropical Forest Science, 7 (1): 10-28

LIESE, W., 1998. The Anatomy of Bamboo Culms. INBAR Technical Report N° 18. International Network for Bamboo and Rattan, Beijing. 204 pp.

LIESE, W. AND GROSSER, D., 2000. An Expanded typology for the Vascular bundles of Bamboo Culms. Proceeding of the BAMBOO 2000 International Symposium. 2-4 August 2000. Chiangmai, Thailand.

LINCOLN, R.J., G.A. BOXSHALL & P.F. CLARK. 1982. A dictionary of ecology, evolution and systematics. Cambridge University Press. Great Britain.

LONDOÑO, X. & L. PRIETO. 1983. Estudio fitoecológico de los guaduales de la zona geográfica del valle del río Cauca. Tesis. Universidad Nacional, Palmira.

LONDOÑO, X. & P. PETERSON. 1992. *Guadua chacoensis* (Poaceae: Bambusoideae), its taxonomic identity, morphology and relationships. Novon 2:41-47.

Londoño, X. 1992. Distribución, morfología, taxonomía, anatomía, silvicultura y usos de los bambúes del Nuevo Mundo. Cespedecia, 19 (62-63): 87-137.

Londoño, X. 1993. Growth Development of *Guadua angustifolia*: a case study in Colombia. Bamboo and its use. *In* International Symposium on industrial use of bamboo, Beijing, China, 7-11 December 1992. International Tropical Timber Organization, Chinese Academy of Forestry. Pag. 80-86.

Londoño, X. 1998. Evaluation of Bamboo Resources in Latin America. Final Report Projetc 96-8300-01-4, INBAR. Sin Publicar.

Londoño, X. 2000. La Guadua, un gigante dormido Pages. 3-5 *in* Memorias Seminario "Guadua en la reconstrucción", Armenia, Colombia, 10-12 Febrero 2000. Editorial Chasqui, Cali.

Londoño, X., G.C. Camayo, N.M. Riaño & Y. Lopez. 2003. Characterization of the anatomy of *Guadua angustifolia* (Poaceae: Bambusoideae) culms. Bamboo, Science and Culture 16. In press.

López L.F. & M.F. Silva. Comportamiento sismoresistente de estructuras de Bahareque. Tesis de Ingeniería Civil. Universidad Nacional de Colombia, sede Manizales. Manizales, 2000. Tesis.

Marulanda, M.L., P. Marquez & X. Londoño. 2003. AFLP analysis of *Guadua angustifolia* (Poaceae: Bambusoideae) in Colombia with emphasis on the Coffee Region. Bamboo, Science and Culture 16. In press.

McClure, F.A. 1966.The Bamboo: A Fresh Perspective. Harvard University Press, Cambridge.

Mejía, J.J. 2000. Eficiencia y costo en la construcción con Guadua, *en* Memorias, Seminario Guadua en la reconstrucción, Armenia, Colombia, Feb.10-12. Pg. 52-53.

Moran, J. 2001. Usos tradicionales y actuales del bambu en America Latina, con énfasis en Colombia y Ecuador. Escuela Politécnica Nacional, Quito, Ecuador.192 pp.

Parsons, J.J. 1991. Giant American bamboo in the vernacular architecture of Colombia and Ecuador. Geographical Review (New York) 81:13-152.

Prieto, E & J. Sánchez. Comportamiento de la *Guadua angustifolia* sometida a flexión. Tesis de Ingeniería Civil. Universidad Nacional, sede Bogotá. Santa Fe de Bogotá, 2001. pp101.

Qisheng, Z. 2000. The bamboo-based board industry in China, *in* International training workshop on sustainable bamboo management and processing techniques for small-size bamboo enterprises, Hangzhou, China, Oct. 4-16, Pg. 63-77.

Riaño, N., X. Londoño, Y. López & J.H. Gómez. 2003. Plant growth and biomass distribution on *Guadua angustifolia* Kunth in relation to ageing in the Valle del Cauca - Colombia. Bamboo Science and Culture 16. In press.

Soderstrom, T.R. & X. Londoño. 1987. Two new genera of Brazilian bamboos related to *Guadua* (Poaceae: Bambusoideae). American Journal of Botany, 74 (1): 27-39.

Soto, H.E. & H. Valencia. 1991. La guadua. Corporación Regional Autónoma de Caldas. División Técnica, sección conservación de suelos y aguas. Manizales, Colombia.

Yongyu, T. 2000. The current status and development trend of bamboo processing in China, *in* International training workshop on sustainable bamboo management and processing techniques for small-size bamboo enterprises, Hangzhou, China, Oct. 4-16, pg. 51-62.

Detail of the Guadua
Pavilion,
Manizales, Caldas,
Colombia.

Glossary

(Spanish or vernacular words and some botanical terms are in italics)

Aliso, a tree (*Alnus jorullensis H.B.K.)* that reaches a height of 30 meters and a diameter of 0.60 meters. It grows in the lower and upper parts of mountain rainforests in light and moist soils. The color of the wood is chestnut to pink. This wood was used for the pillars of the Guadua Pavilion in Expo-Hannover 2000

Alluvial, terrain formed by the deposits left by floods or rivers.

Bahareque of bamboo/guadua, a constructional system in which thin, strong walls are obtained by placing bamboo/guadua props equidistantly on a frame of wood or bamboo that is covered internally and externally with a matting of bamboo splits (see: *Esterilla).*

Bamba, a tabular root.

Biomass, any quantitative estimate of the total mass of live organisms that make up all or part of a population or any other specific unit, or within a given area at a given time.

Cantilever, a horizontal projection, such as a roof, balcony or beam, supported at one end only.

Caoba Palo Santo, big-leafed Mahogany (*Swietenia macrophylla*), a tree which reaches a height of 45 meters and a diameter of 2 meters. It has a straight and cylindrical trunk and grows in dry and humid tropical forests. It has a yellowish color with a pronounced grain which varies from creamy pink to dark red-brown.

Cauline leaf, large, modified and superposed leaves that protect the young shoots in woody bamboos. The leaf consists of a sheath, lamina and internal ligule. They may be persistent but they generally fall off with the development of the branches.

Cedro, a variety of cedar (*Cedrela angustifolia* Mociño & Sessé ex DC.) , which may reach a height of 60 meters and a diameter of 1.5 meters. It has a straight, cylindrical trunk and grows in dry and humid tropical forests. The color of its wood varies from yellowish pink to reddish brown.

Cespitose, Growing in dense tufts or clumps. Describes bamboos whose rhizomes are "clumping" as opposed to "running", and which therefore do not tend to develop along the surface of the soil.

Chromosomal number, the number of chromosomes that is characteristic of a given organism. Chromosomes contain the genetic material of an organism.

Culm, Bamboo cane or stem. The segmented aerial axis that emerges from a rhizome.

Deciduous, that which falls off when it matures. In bamboos it refers to the cauline leaves, foliar leaves and floscules of the spikelets.

Ecotype, A locally-adapted population; an infraspecific race or group with distinctive characters, resulting from the selective pressure of local or environmental conditions: a subunit within an ecospecies.

Above, left
Spanish colonial "par y nudillo" structure. Restoration of the "Casa del Estanco" (Office of the Spanish Crown tobacco monopoly). Cartagena, Bolívar, Colombia. Luis Restrepo.

Above, right
In contrast with the traditional Spanish "par y nudillo", which has a powerful wooden tensor to counteract the horizontal thrusts against the walls, Simón Vélez compensates for this thrust with large cantilevers, eliminating the tensors. No horizontal element crosses the interior vault.

Above
Mock-up of structure of main bedroom. Isla Canales de Tierra, Central America. Design: Simón Vélez.

Edaphic, pertaining to or influenced by the nature of the soil.

Endemic, native and restricted to a particular geographical region.

Entomofauna, the group of insects that inhabit a territory.

Epithet, in taxonomy, the second word of the binomial name of a species.

Esterilla, A matting of bamboo splits, used as a construction material, made of canes that are split lengthwise and flattened.

Floscule, the unit of a spikelet of bamboo or other *gramineae*; consists of a unisexual or bisexual flower enclosed in a palea, which is enclosed, in turn, by the lemma.

Foliage lamina, in the woody bamboos, the leaves of the branches of the culm, with a well-developed green lamina and a small sheath. They live longer than the cauline leaves.

Foliar, pertaining to leaves

Genus, the category of biological classification that includes one or more individuals phylogenetically related and morphologically similar; a rank in the hierarchy of taxonomic classification between the family and the species. It is assumed that the members of one genus are closer to one another phylogenetically than to any species of another genus.

Gramineae, the grass family

Gregarious flowering, a pattern of flowering in which all the individuals of a species flower at the same time and then die.

Habit, the external appearance, aspect or form of growth of an organism.

Habitat, site or place occupied by an organism: local environment.

Herbaceous, a plant which has non-lignified stalks and dies annually.

Keel, the ridge that is formed when a structure like the palea, lemma or a foliar sheath coils in its longitudinal direction. Generally a nerve is present along the length of the keel.

Macana, duramen or heartwood of palm.

Miocene, geological epoch within the Tertiary period (approximately 23-5 million years ago).

Monocarpic, that which produces a single fruit or only has one period of fruition during its life cycle.

Nato, (*Mora megistosperma (Pittier) Britton & Rose*) , a tree which reaches a height of 26 meters and a diameter of 1 meter. It has an upright, cylindrical or irregular trunk, with long tabular roots. The wood has a rosy-white color with an abrupt transition to red with a dark brown tinge. It needs the influence of salt and sweet water, for this reason it is found at the mouths of rivers that flow into the sea, near mangrove swamps.

Nogal, (*Cordia alliodora* Ruiz & Pavón) a tree which reaches a height of 35 meters and a diameter of 0.9 meters, with a straight trunk. The color of the wood is yellow or pale golden brown. Very common in the coffee zone, where it used for carpentry and furniture.

Oligocene, geological epoch within the Tertiary period (approximately 38 to 26 million years ago).

Pachymorph, a type of rhizome in which the internodes are more wide than long, asymmetrical and solid: the end of each rhizome curves upwards to form the aerial culm

Palea, the upper bract which encloses the flower of the Gramineae. It normally has two keels and two veins, or in the case of the bamboos, a large number of veins

Páramo, high Andean moorland (from 3,000 meters to 5,000 above sea level), with a plant community characterized by tussock grasses, large rosette plants, shrubs with evergreen, coriaceous and sclerophyllous leaves, and cushion plants.

Par y nudillo, structural element of a two-slope roof, characteristic of Spanish colonial architecture in Colombia, that is formed by two beams that meet at the vertex (*"pares"*) and a transversal element (*"nudillo"*) that is placed about a third of the way up the roof.

Perennial, plants that live for several years with periods of annual growth.

Poaceae, within the taxonomic classification of plants, the family to which the *Gramineae* belong.

Pseudo-spikelet, the unit of inflorescence of many woody bamboos, which branches from the axis of its own basal bract.

Rhizome, a subterranean culm or part of the culm with nodes and internodes; it shows rootlets and leaves in the form of scales on the nodes; consists of the neck and the rhizome itself.

Sapán, (*Clathrotropis brachypetala* (Tul.)Kleinhoonte), a tree which grows to a height of 35 meters and a diameter of 0.9 meters. It has a straight and cylindrical trunk and grows in the tropical rainforest. Its sapwood is a clear pink color with an abrupt transition to a heartwood of dark or light chestnut, at times with conspicuous stains of yellowish chestnut, and with fine grains. A timber of strong physical and mechanical properties, it is difficult to work and has a high finish. Its density is close to 1.0.

Seismic-resistant, unaffected by telluric movements

Shoot, In bamboos the first state of development of the culm, recognizable when it is covered by cauline leaves.

Species, a group of organisms, minerals or other entities formally recognized to be distinct from other groups. The basic unit of biological classification; the category below genus in the hierarchy of classification.

Spikelet, basic unit in the inflorescence of the bamboos and other *Gramineae* ; generally consists of 2 or more glumes and one or many floscules arranged along the rachis.

Sporadic, that which occurs in an occasional manner: applied to the uncertain flowering of the bamboos.

Stamen, the masculine part of the flower which contains the pollen; consists of the filament and anther.

Stigma, the terminal branch (es) of the pistil where pollen is deposited.

Stomata, microscopic pores on the leaves and other organs of the bamboo and other *Gramineae*, through which occurs the exchange of gases during photosynthesis

Style, the upper part of the ovary of the flower, which ends in one or several stigmas.

Sub-tribe, the rank in taxonomic classification immediately after the tribe.

Sympodial, a type of ramification in which each successive branch is dominant.

Taxa, includes several taxonomic genera.

Tertiary, Tertiary or Cenozoic era: began 65 million years ago and lasted for approximately 60 million years.

Lectern
Gilberto Jaramillo
Taller Cantarrana.
Neira, Colombia.

Opposite page
Walking sticks
Gilberto Jaramillo
Taller Cantarrana.
Neira, Colombia.